Tucholsky Wagner Zola Scott Sydow Freud Schlegel
Turgenev Fonatne Wallace
Twain Walther von der Vogelweide Fouqué Friedrich II. von Preußen
Weber Freiligrath Frey
Fechner Fichte Weiße Rose von Fallersleben Kant Ernst Frommel
Richthofen
Hölderlin
Engels Fielding Eichendorff Tacitus Dumas
Fehrs Faber Flaubert
Eliasberg Ebner Eschenbach
Feuerbach Maximilian I. von Habsburg Fock Eliot Zweig
Ewald Vergil
Goethe London
Mendelssohn Balzac Shakespeare Elisabeth von Österreich Dostojewski Ganghofer
Trackl Stevenson Lichtenberg Rathenau Doyle Gjellerup
Mommsen Tolstoi Hambruch
Thoma Lenz Hanrieder Droste-Hülshoff
Dach Verne von Arnim Hägele Hauff Humboldt
Karrillon Reuter Rousseau Hagen Hauptmann Gautier
Garschin Defoe Baudelaire
Damaschke Descartes Hebbel
Hegel Kussmaul Herder
Wolfram von Eschenbach Dickens Schopenhauer Rilke George
Bronner Darwin Melville Grimm Jerome
Campe Horváth Aristoteles Bebel Proust
Bismarck Vigny Voltaire Federer Herodot
Gengenbach Barlach Heine
Storm Casanova Tersteegen Grillparzer Georgy
Chamberlain Lessing Langbein Gilm Gryphius
Brentano Lafontaine
Strachwitz Claudius Schiller Kralik Iffland Sokrates
Katharina II. von Rußland Bellamy Schilling
Gerstäcker Raabe Gibbon Tschechow
Löns Hesse Hoffmann Gogol Wilde Gleim Vulpius
Luther Heym Hofmannsthal Morgenstern
Roth Klee Hölty Goedicke
Luxemburg Heyse Klopstock Kleist
Puschkin Homer Mörike
Machiavelli La Roche Horaz Musil
Navarra Aurel Musset Kierkegaard Kraft Kraus
Lamprecht Kind Kirchhoff Hugo Moltke
Nestroy Marie de France
Laotse Ipsen Liebknecht
Nietzsche Nansen
Marx Lassalle Gorki Klett Leibniz Ringelnatz
von Ossietzky
May vom Stein Lawrence Irving
Petalozzi Knigge
Platon Pückler Michelangelo Kafka
Sachs Poe Kock
Liebermann
de Sade Praetorius Mistral Zetkin Korolenko

The publishing house tredition has created the series **TREDITION CLASSICS**. It contains classical literature works from over two thousand years. Most of these titles have been out of print and off the bookstore shelves for decades.

The book series is intended to preserve the cultural legacy and to promote the timeless works of classical literature. As a reader of a **TREDITION CLASSICS** book, the reader supports the mission to save many of the amazing works of world literature from oblivion.

The symbol of **TREDITION CLASSICS** is Johannes Gutenberg (1400 – 1468), the inventor of movable type printing.

With the series, tredition intends to make thousands of international literature classics available in printed format again – worldwide.

All books are available at book retailers worldwide in paperback and in hardcover. For more information please visit: www.tredition.com

tredition was established in 2006 by Sandra Latusseck and Soenke Schulz. Based in Hamburg, Germany, tredition offers publishing solutions to authors and publishing houses, combined with worldwide distribution of printed and digital book content. tredition is uniquely positioned to enable authors and publishing houses to create books on their own terms and without conventional manufacturing risks.

For more information please visit: www.tredition.com

In Ancient Albemarle

Catherine Albertson

Imprint

This book is part of the TREDITION CLASSICS series.

Author: Catherine Albertson
Cover design: toepferschumann, Berlin (Germany)

Publisher: tredition GmbH, Hamburg (Germany)
ISBN: 978-3-8491-8715-6

www.tredition.com
www.tredition.de

OLD FLOAT BRIDGE ACROSS THE PERQUIMANS RIVER

DEDICATION

To

Mary Hilliard Hinton

State Regent Daughters of the Revolution

without whose aid and encouragement

these chapters would never

have been written

—C.A.

THE PERQUIMANS RIVER

From the Great Swamp's mysterious depths,
Where wild beasts lurk and strange winds sough;
From ancient forests dense and dark,
Where gray moss wreathes the cypress bough;
'Mid marshes green with flowers starred,
Through fens where reeds and rushes sway,
Past fertile fields of waving grain,
Down to the sea I take my way.

The wild swan floats upon my breast;
The sea-gulls to my waters sink;
And stealing to my low green shores,
The timid deer oft stoops to drink.
The yellow jessamine's golden bells
Ring on my banks their fairy chime;
And tall flag lilies bow and bend,
To the low music keeping time.

Between my narrow, winding banks,
For many a mile I dream along
'Mid silence deep, unbroken save
By rustling reed, or wild bird's song;
Or murmuring of my shadowed waves
Beneath the feathery cypress trees,
Or pines, responsive to the breath
Of winds that breathe sea memories.

So far removed seem shore and stream,
From sound and sight of mart or mill,
That Kilcokonen's painted braves
Might roam my woods and marshes still.
And still, as in the days of yore,
Ere yet the white man's sail I knew,
Upon my amber waves might skim
The Indian maiden's light canoe.

Thus, half asleep, I dream along,
Till low at first, and far away,
Then louder, more insistent, calls
A voice my heart would fain obey.
And by a force resistless drawn,
The narrow banks that fetter me
I thrust apart, and onward sweep
In quiet strength toward the sea.

I leave my marshes and my fens;
I dream no more upon my way;
But forward press, a river grown,
In the great world my part to play.
Upon my wide and ample breast,
The white-winged boats go hurrying by;
And on my banks the whirring wheels
Of busy mills hum ceaselessly.

And sharing man's incessant toil,
I journey ever onward down,
With many a lovely sister stream,
With all the waters of the Sound,
To join the sea, whose billows break,
In silver spray, in wild uproar,
Upon the golden bars that guard
The lonely Carolina shore.

CONTENTS

ILLUSTRATIONS

IN ANCIENT ALBEMARLE

CHAPTER I

WIKACOME IN WEAPOMEIOK, THE HOME OF GEORGE DURANT

In Perquimans County, North Carolina, there lies between the beautiful Perquimans River on the west, and her fair and placid sister, the Katoline or Little River, on the east, a lovely strip of land to which the red man in days long gone, gave the name of Wikacome. The broad sound whose tawny waters wash the southern shores of this peninsula, as well as all that tract of land lying between the Chowan River and the Atlantic Ocean, were known to the primitive dwellers in that region as Weapomeiok.

Not until George Durant came into Carolina, and following him a thin stream of settlers that finally overflowed the surrounding country, did the beautiful Indian names give place to those by which they are now known. Then Wikacome became the familiar Durant's Neck, and the waters of Weapomeiok and the territory known to the aborigines by the same name, changed to the historic cognomen of Albemarle.

George Durant and Samuel Pricklove were the first of the Anglo-Saxon race to establish a permanent settlement in Wikacome, though they were not the first Englishmen whose eyes had rested upon its virgin forests and fair green meadows, for in the early spring of 1586 Ralph Lane, who had been sent with Sir Richard Grenville by Sir Walter Raleigh to colonize Roanoke Island, set out with fourteen comrades from that place on an exploring expedition, hoping to find the golden "Will-o'-the-Wisp," which led so many English adventurers of the day to seek their fortunes in the New World.

As far as the Roanoke River sailed the bold explorer and his comrades, among whom were Philip Amadas and the historian Hakluyt. To the south as far as Craven County they pushed their little boat, and northward to the shores of Chesapeake Bay. In the course of their journey they touched at Chepanock, an Indian village lying at the extremity of Durant's Neck. And Lane relates that on his return trip he stopped again at that point to secure a supply of provisions, and to fish in the sound.

It was Easter morning, 1586, when Lane and his hardy sailors, worn out from their rough voyage down the Chowan and up the tawny waters of the sound, sailed into the quiet harbor of the Katoline River. Half starved, for the hostile tribes of the Mangoaks on the Chowan River, after being repulsed in an attack upon the strangers, had refused to sell them food, Lane and his men, for two days without means of staying their hunger, hoped to buy from the Indians of Weapomeiok the provisions so sorely needed.

But when the little band of explorers rowed their small craft to the shore, and set out in search of corn and meat, they found the wigwams of Chepanock deserted, and no sign of the red men. The Indians doubtless had been alarmed at the sight of the strangers when they first stopped at the village, and had fled from their homes to the interior of the country.

No corn nor meal could Lane procure, but the weirs were full of fish, and the men were able to satisfy their hunger, and having rested at Chepanock that night they returned to Roanoke Island next morning. When the plash of their oars died away in the distance, the waters of the Katoline and the northern shores of Weapomeiok knew the white man's sails no more until over half a century had passed away.

Lane and his colony, discouraged in their hopes of finding gold, and disheartened by the many misfortunes that had befallen them, sailed back to England with Sir Francis Drake. Raleigh's second attempt a year later to establish a colony on Roanoke Island ended in the pathetic story of little Virginia Dare and the "Lost Colony." Queen Elizabeth died, and the tyrannical reign of James I came to an end. Charles I and Cromwell waged their bitter war; the Commonwealth and Protectorate ran their brief course, and the Restoration of 1660 brought back the third of the Stuarts to the throne of England.

During all these changes in the ownership of Carolina and her sister colonies, the red man roamed unmolested through the forests of

Wikacome and fished the weirs in the silver streams flowing into the broad waters of Weapomeiok, unafraid of the great, white-winged boats of the pale face. These brief visits to his shores were now remembered only when the tribes gathered around the great camp fires at night, and listened to the tales told by ancient braves and squaws, to whom the appearance of the swift ships of the strangers now seemed only a dim, half-remembered dream.

But as the years rolled by, venturesome hunters and trappers from Virginia began to thread their way through the tangled woods of the region lying to the south of the Chesapeake. Returning to their homes they carried with them glowing accounts of the mild climate, the placid streams teeming with fish, the wild game and rich furs to be found in the country through which they had wandered.

In 1630 Sir Robert Heath, to whom Charles I granted a large portion of Carolina, attempted to establish a settlement in the territory. Later Roger Green, an English clergyman, made a similar attempt near the present town of Edenton, but both these efforts failed. However, the spirit of discovery and adventure was now fully aroused, and by 1656 a number of settlements had been established along the shores of the streams that flow into Albemarle Sound. Of none of these, however, can any accurate account be given, their date and location having long been forgotten; and not until 1661 is there any authenticated record of a permanent settlement in North Carolina.

A year or two previous to that date, George Durant, a planter from Virginia, attracted by the enthusiastic accounts he had heard of the desirable lands to be found lying to the south, started out on an exploring expedition to see for himself if all he had heard of the Indian land of Weapomeiok were true, intending, if the country came up to his expectations, there to establish his home.

For nearly two years Durant journeyed through the country, and finally satisfied that the glowing accounts he had heard were not exaggerated, he determined to bring his wife and family, his goods and chattels, into this new "Land of Promise," and there build for himself a house to dwell in, and to clear away the forest for a plantation. The first spot selected by him for his future home was very near the ancient Indian village of Chepanock, on the peninsula of Wikacome, which juts out into the wide waters of Weapomeiok, and whose shores are watered by the Katoline and the Perquimans rivers.

With the coming of George Durant to Carolina, the old Indian name Wikacome vanishes from history, and "Durant's Neck" becomes the name by which that section is henceforth known. The sound and the region north of it, first known as Weapomeiok, change to Albemarle; and the Katoline River soon loses its Indian designation, and is known to the settlers who made their homes on its banks as the "Little River."

With the establishment of George Durant on the peninsula now called by his name, the connected history of North Carolina begins. And it is a matter of pride to the citizens of the Old North State that our first settler, with a sturdy honesty and a sense of justice shown but seldom to the red man by the pioneers in the colonies, bought from the Indian chief, Kilcokonen "for a valuable consideration" the land on which he established his home. The deed for this tract of land is now in the old court-house in Hertford, North Carolina, and is the earliest recorded in the history of our State. The following is an exact copy of this ancient document:

"George Durant's Deed
from
Kilcokonen:

"Know all men these Presents that I, Kilcokonen King of the Yeopems have for a valuable consideration of satisfaction received with ye consent of my People sold and made over and delivered to George Durant, a Parcel of land lying and being on a river called by ye name of Perquimans, which issueth out of the North side of the aforesaid Sound, and which land at present bears ye name of Wecameke. Beginning at a marked oak tree which divideth this land from ye land I formerly sold Samuel Precklove and extending easterly up ye said Sound at a point or turning of ye aforesaid Perquimans River and so up ye east side of ye said river to a creek called Awoseake to wit, all ye land between ye aforesaid bounds of Samuel Precklove and the said creek whence to ye head thereof. And thence through ye woods to ye first bounds. To have and to hold ye quiet possession of ye same to him, his heirs forever, with all rights and privileges thereto forever from me or any person or persons whatsoever, as witness my hand this first day of March 1661.

"KILCOKONEN.

"Test: Thos Weamouth, Caleb Callaway."

Having thus fairly and justly bought his lands, as this and other deeds from Kilcokonen testify, Durant proceeded to establish his belongings on his estate, and to take up the strenuous life of a pioneer in a new country.

And a fairer region never gladdened the eyes of men making a new home in a strange land. In the virgin forests surrounding the settlers' homes, the crimson berried holly tree against the dark background of lofty pines brightened the winter landscape. The opulent Southern spring flung wide the white banners of dogwood, enriched the forest aisles with fretted gold of jessamine and scarlet of coral honeysuckle, and spread the ground with carpet of velvet moss, of rosy azaleas and blue-eyed innocents. The wide rivers that flow in placid beauty by the wooded banks of ancient Wikacome, formed a highway for the commerce of the settlers and a connecting link with the outer sea. And however fierce and bold the wild creatures of those dark forests might be, the teeming fish and game of the surrounding woods and waters kept far from the settlers' doors the wolf of want and hunger.

The fame of this fertile spot spread, and ere long George Durant was greeting many newcomers into the country. Samuel Pricklove had preceded him into Wikacome, and later came George Catchmaid, Captain John Hecklefield and Richard Sanderson, while later still the Blounts, the Whedbees, the Newbys, Harveys and Skinners, names still prominent in Albemarle, came into the neighborhood and settled throughout Perquimans County.

At the homes of the planters on Durant's Neck the public business of the Albemarle Colony was for many years transacted. Courts were held, councils convened, and assemblies called, while from the wharves of the planters on Little River and the Perquimans, white-sailed vessels carried the produce of the rich fields and dense forests to New England, to the West Indies and to the mother country.

Many of the most interesting events in the early history of Albemarle occurred on Durant's Neck. The Culpeper Rebellion, of which George Durant and John Culpeper were among the leaders, began in Pasquotank, but reached its culmination in Durant's home on Little River. There, also, Thomas Miller was imprisoned for a time, and there the leaders of the rebellion organized a new people's government, the first in the New World absolutely independent of Proprietors, Parliament and King. At Hecklefield's home on Little River, the plantation adjoining Durant's, the Assembly of 1708 met to investigate the Cary-Glover question and to decide which of those two claimants to the gubernatorial chair had rightful authority to occupy that exalted seat. There also George Eden was sworn in as ruler of North Carolina under the Proprietors; and there the death of Queen Anne was announced to the Governor's Council, and George I was formally proclaimed true and lawful sovereign of Carolina.

A prominent meeting place for the courts, councils and assemblies in Colonial Albemarle was the home of Captain Richard Sanderson in the Little River settlement on Durant's Neck. Of the many notable events that occurred at the home of this wealthy and influential planter, probably the Assembly of 1715 leads in interest and importance. The acts passed by this Assembly were directed to be printed, but the order was evidently never carried out, as none but manuscript copies are now extant.

Among the most important measures taken by this Assembly was one making the Church of England the established Church of the Colony; though freedom of worship was granted to all, and the Quakers were allowed to substitute a solemn affirmation in lieu of an oath. Other acts, necessary to the welfare of the Colony, were passed, and a revision of all former acts was made. Edward Moseley, Speaker of the House, was of course present on this occasion, as were Governor Eden, Thomas Byrd, of Pasquotank, Tobias Knight, of Currituck, Christopher Gale, of Chowan, and Maurice Moore, of Perquimans.

Of all these old homes on Durant's Neck where so much of the early history of our State was made, none are now standing; though the sites of several of these historic places are well known to the dwellers on the peninsula. When the tide is low on Little River, the bricks of what was once the home of Governor Drummond can be seen. And an old tombstone found in the sound, which is now used as the lower step of the side porch in a beautiful old home, on Durant's Neck, once the property of Mr. Edward Leigh, but now owned by Mr. C.W. Grandy, of Norfolk, is said to have once marked the grave of Seth Sothel. The inscription on the stone is now obliterated, but the original owners of the home declared that the old inhabitants of Durant's Neck claimed that the slab at one time bore the name of this, the most infamous of all the unworthy Governors whom the Proprietors placed over the people of Albemarle.

The site of Durant's home is well known, and until a few years ago a tombstone bearing his name, it is said, was standing under an old sweet-gum tree on the bank of a great ditch near the sound. But the field hands in clearing the ditch undermined the stone and covered it with earth, so it now lies hidden from view.

But though no monument now marks the resting place of our first settler, George Durant, there is no need of "storied urn or animated bust" to keep alive in the hearts of his countrymen the memory of his name, and of the brave, fearless spirit which made him a tower of strength to the Old North State in the struggles of her early days.

CHAPTER II

THE FIRST ALBEMARLE ASSEMBLY—HALL'S CREEK NEAR NIXONTON

In 1653 King Charles II granted to eight noblemen of his court a tract of land reaching from the northern shores of Albemarle Sound to St. John's River in Florida, and from the Atlantic Ocean to the Pacific Ocean. A small strip extending from the north shore of the Albemarle Sound to the southern boundary of Virginia was not included in this grant, but nevertheless the Lords Proprietors, of whom Governor Berkeley, of Virginia, was one, assumed control over this section; and in 1663 these noblemen authorized Berkeley to appoint a governor to rule over this territory, whose ownership was a disputed question for several years.

In 1665 the Albemarle region, as it came to be called, comprising the four ancient counties of Currituck, Pasquotank, Perquimans and Chowan, had become very valuable on account of the rich plantations established therein by such men as George Durant, of Perquimans, and Valentine Byrd, of Pasquotank; and the Lords Proprietors, as the owners of the Carolinas were called, begged the king to include the above-named strip of land in their grant. This the king did, ignorant of the vast extent of the territory which he had already bestowed upon the Lords.

William Drummond, whom Berkeley, of Virginia, had appointed to govern this Albemarle country, came into Carolina in 1664, and assumed the reins of government. To assist him in his arduous duties, the Lords authorized Berkeley to appoint six of the most prominent men in the settlement to form what came to be known as the Governor's Council. This body of men, with the Governor, acted for many years as the judicial department of the State, and also corresponded to what is now the Senate Chamber in our legislative department.

That the liberty-loving pioneers in Carolina might feel that they were a self-governing people, every free man in the settlement was to have right of membership in the General Assembly, which was to meet yearly to enact the laws. After the Governor, Councilors, and the freemen or their deputies had passed the laws, a copy of them was to be sent to the Lords for their consideration. Should they meet with the approval of the Proprietors, they went into effect; if not, they were null and void.

In the fall of 1664, Governor Drummond began organizing the government of his new province; and on February 6, 1665, the "Grand Assembly of Albemarle," as these early law-makers styled themselves, met to frame a set of laws for this Albemarle Colony. The place chosen for the meeting of this first legislative body ever assembled in our State, was a little knoll overlooking Hall's Creek in Pasquotank County, about a mile from Nixonton, a small town which was chartered nearly a hundred years later.

No record of the names of these hardy settlers who were present at this Grand Assembly has been handed down to us; but on such an important occasion we may be sure that all the prominent men in the Albemarle region who could attend would make it a point to do so.

George Drummond and his secretary, Thomas Woodward, were surely there; George Durant, Samuel Pricklove, John Harvey, all owners of great plantations in Perquimans, doubtless were on hand. Thomas Raulfe, Timothy Biggs, Valentine Byrd, Solomon Poole, all large landowners in Pasquotank, must have been there; Thomas Jarvis, of Currituck, and Thomas Pollock, of Chowan, may have represented their counties. And all—the dignified, reserved Scotch Governor, his haughty secretary, the wealthy, influential planters and the humble farmers and hunters—must have felt the solemnity of the occasion and recognized its importance.

We may imagine the scene: Under the spreading boughs of a lordly oak, this group of men were gathered. Around them the dark forest stretched, the wind murmuring in the pines and fragrant with the aromatic odor of the spicy needles. At a distance a group of red men, silent and immovable, some with bow and arrow in hand, leaning against the trees, others sitting on the ground, gazed with wondering eyes upon the palefaces assembled for their first great pow-wow.

Down at the foot of the knoll the silver waves of the creek rippled softly against the shore; on its waters the sloops of the planters from

the settlements nearby; here and there on its bosom, an Indian canoe moored close to its shores.

As to the work accomplished by this first Albemarle Assembly,
only one fact is certain, and that is the drawing up by the members
of a petition to the Lords Proprietors, begging that these settlers in
Carolina should be allowed to hold their lands on the same conditions and terms as the people of Virginia. The Lords graciously
consented to this petition, and on the 1st of May, 1668, they issued a
paper known to this day as the Deed of Grant, by which land in
Albemarle was directed to be granted on the same terms as in Virginia. The deed was duly recorded in Albemarle, and was preserved with scrupulous care.

There is a tradition in the county that the Assembly also took
steps for preparing for an Indian war then threatening, which broke
out the following year, but was soon suppressed.

Doubtless other laws were enacted, such as were necessary for
the settlement, though no record of them is extant. And then, the
business that called them together having been transacted, and the
wheels of government set in motion, these early law-makers returned home, to manor house and log cabin, to the care of the great
plantations, to the plow, and the wild, free life of the hunter and
trapper; and a new government had been born.

There seems to be no doubt in the minds of such historians as
Colonel Saunders, Captain Ashe, and President D.H. Hill, that the
first Albemarle Assembly did convene in the early spring of 1665.
As for the day and month, tradition alone is our authority. An old
almanac of H.D. Turner's gives the date as February 6th, and in
default of any more certain date, this was inscribed upon the tablet
which the Sir Walter Raleigh Chapter Daughters of the Revolution
have erected at Hall's Creek Church.

As to the statement that the place marked by the tablet was the
scene of the meeting of our first assemblymen, tradition again is
responsible. But such authorities as Captain Ashe, and various
members of the State Historical Commission, accept the tradition as
a fact. And all old residents of Nixonton assert that their fathers and
grandfathers handed the story down to them.

An extract from a letter from Captain Ashe, author of Ashe's History of North Carolina, to the Regent of the local Chapter Daughters of the Revolution may be of interest here:

"Yesterday I came across in the library at Washington, this entry, made by the late Mrs. Frances Hill, widow of Secretary of the State William Hill: 'I was born in Nixonton March 14, 1789. Nixonton is a small town one mile from Hall's Creek, and on a little rise of ground from the bridge stood the big oak, where the first settlers of our county held their assembly.'"

Other documents in possession of the Regent of our local Chapter Daughters of the Revolution go to show that the place and date as named on the tablet at Hall's Creek are authentic, and that Pasquotank County may claim with truth the honor of having been the scene of the first meeting of the Grand Assembly of Albemarle.

CHAPTER III

ENFIELD FARM—WHERE THE CULPEPER REBELLION BEGAN

Some two or three miles south of Elizabeth City on the banks of the Pasquotank River, just where that lovely stream suddenly broadens out into a wide and beautiful expanse, lies the old plantation known in our county from earliest days as Enfield Farm, sometimes Winfield.

It is hard to trace the original owners of the plantation, but the farm is probably part of the original patent granted in 1663 by Sir William Berkeley, one of the Lords Proprietors, to Mr. Thomas Relfe, "on account of his bringing into the colony fifteen persons and paying on St. Michael's Day, the 29th of September, one shilling for every acre of land."

On this plantation, close to the river shore, was erected about 1670, according to our local tradition, the home of the planter, two rooms of which are still standing and in good preservation. Possibly "Thomas Relfe, Gentleman," as he is styled in the Colonial Records, was the builder of this relic of bygone days, whose massive brick walls and stout timbers have for so long defied the onslaughts of time.

Many are the stories, legendary and historical, that have gathered around this ancient building. Among the most interesting of the latter is that connected with the Culpeper Rebellion, an event as important in North Carolina history as Bacon's Rebellion is in the history of Virginia.

The cause of Culpeper's Rebellion dates back to the passing of the navigation act by Cromwell's Parliament, when that vigorous ruler held sway in England and over the American colonies. This act, later broadened and amended, finally prohibited the colonists not only from importing goods from Europe unless they were shipped from England, but forbade the use of any but English vessels in the carrying trade; and finally declared that inter-colonial trade should cease, and that England alone should be the market for the buying and selling of goods on the part of the Americans. Naturally the colonies objected to such a selfish restriction of their trade, and naturally there was much smuggling carried on, wherever and whenever this avoidance of the navigation acts could be made in safety.

To none of these thirteen colonies were these laws more injurious than to the infant settlement on the northern shores of Albemarle Sound in Carolina. The sand bars along the coast prevented the establishment of a seaport from whence trade could be carried on with the mother country. The large, English-built vessels could not pass through the shallow inlets that connect the Atlantic with the Carolina inland waterways. To have strictly obeyed the laws passed by the British Parliament would have been the death blow to the commerce and to the prosperity of the Albemarle settlement. So, for about fifteen years after George Durant bought his tract of land on Durant's Neck from Kilcokonen, the great chief of the Yeopims, the planters in Albemarle had paid but little attention to the trade laws. The Proprietors appointed no customs collectors in the little colony, and had not considered it worth while to interfere with the trade which the shrewd New Englanders had built up in Carolina.

Enterprising Yankee shipbuilders, realizing their opportunity, constructed staunch little vessels which could weather the seas, sail over to Europe, load up with goods necessary to the planter, return and glide down the coast till they found an opening between the dreaded bars, then, slipping from sound to sound, carry to the planters in the Albemarle region the cargoes for which they were waiting.

Another law requiring payment of an export tax on tobacco, then the principal crop of the Albemarle sections, as it was of Virginia, was evaded for many years by the settlers in this region. Governors Drummond and Stevens, and John Judkins, president of the council, must have known of this disregard of the laws, both on the part of the Yankee shippers and the Albemarle planters. But realizing that too strict an adherence to England's trade laws would mean ruin to the colonists, these officers were conveniently blind to the illegal proceedings of their people.

But after the organization of the board of trade in London, of which four of the Proprietors were members, the rulers of Carolina determined to enforce the laws more strictly among their subjects in far-away Carolina. So Timothy Biggs, of the Little River Settlement, was appointed surveyor of customs, and Valentine Byrd, of Pasquotank, collector of customs, with orders to enforce the navigation acts and other trade laws, so long disregarded.

There was violent opposition to this decision of the Lords, as was to have been expected; but finally the settlers were persuaded to allow the officers to perform their duty. Valentine Byrd, himself, one of the wealthiest and most influential men in Albemarle, was by no means rigid or exacting in collecting the tobacco tax; and for several years longer, though the laws were ostensibly observed, numerous ways were found to evade them. The colonists, however, were by no means satisfied; for though they were successful in avoiding a strict adherence to the laws, and in continuing their trade with New England, still the fact that the hated acts were in force at all, was to them a thorn in the flesh.

Matters soon reached a crisis, and the smouldering feeling of resentment against the Proprietors broke out into open rebellion. In 1676 the Lords appointed Thomas Eastchurch Governor of Albemarle and Thomas Miller collector of customs for that settlement. Both of these men, who were then in London, had previously lived in Albemarle and had incurred the enmity of some of the leading men in the settlement, Eastchurch especially being in bad repute among the planters.

In 1677, Eastchurch and Miller departed from London to take up their duties in Carolina. Stopping at the Island of Nevis on their way over, Eastchurch became enamored of the charms (and the fortune) of a fair Creole who there abode, and dallied on the island until he succeeded in winning the lady's hand. Miller, whom Eastchurch appointed his deputy in Carolina, continued on his way alone. When he reached Albemarle, the people received him kindly and allowed him to fill Eastchurch's place. But no sooner had he assumed the reins of government than he began a rigid enforcement of the trade and navigation laws. Of course the planters resented his activity in this direction, and most bitterly did they resent his compelling a strict payment of the tobacco tax. Possibly, however, no open rebellion would have occurred, had not Miller proceeded to high-handed and arbitrary deeds, making himself so obnoxious to the people that finally they were wrought up to such an inflammable state of mind that only a spark was needed to light the flames of revolution.

And that spark was kindled in December, 1677, when Captain Zachary Gilliam, a shrewd New England shipmaster, came into the colony in his trig little vessel, "The Carolina," bringing with him, besides the supplies needed by the planters for the winter days at hand, ammunition and firearms which a threatened Indian uprising made necessary for the safety of the settlers' homes.

On board the "Carolina" was George Durant, the first settler in the colony, and the acknowledged leader in public affairs in Albemarle. He had been over to England to consult the Lords Proprietors concerning matters relating to the colony, and was returning to his home on Durant's Neck.

Through the inlet at Ocracoke the "Carolina" slipped, over the broad waters of Pamlico Sound, past Roanoke Island, home of Virginia Dare, and into Albemarle Sound. Then up the blue waters of the Pasquotank she sailed, with "Jack ancient flag and pennant flying," as Miller indignantly relates, till she came to anchor at Captain Crawford's landing, just off the shore from Enfield Farm.

Gladly did the bluff captain and the jovial planter row ashore from their sea-tossed berths. Many were the friendly greetings extended them, both prime favorites among the settlers, who came hurrying down to Enfield when the news of the "Carolina's" arrival spread through the community. Eager questions assailed them on every side concerning news of loved ones in the mother country; and a busy day did Captain Gilliam put in, chaffering and bargaining with the planters who anxiously surrounded him in quest of long needed supplies.

Durant, though doubtless impatient to proceed as quickly as possible to his home and family in Perquimans, nevertheless spent the day pleasantly enough talking to his brother planters, Valentine Byrd, Samuel Pricklove, and others. All was going merrily as a marriage bell when suddenly Deputy Governor Miller appeared on the scene, accused Gilliam of having contraband goods on board, and of having evaded the export tax on tobacco when he sailed out of port with his cargo a year before. A violent altercation arose, in which the planters, with few exceptions, sided with Gilliam, who indignantly (if not quite truthfully) denied the charges brought against him.

Miller at last withdrew, muttering imprecations and threats against Gilliam; but about 10 o'clock that night he returned with several government officials, boarded the "Carolina" and attempted to arrest both Gilliam and Durant. The planters, among whom were Valentine Byrd, Captain Crawford, Captain Jenkins and John Culpeper, hearing of the disturbance, anxious for the safety of their friends, and fearing lest Gilliam should sail away before they had concluded their purchases, came hurrying in hot haste to the rescue. Rowing swiftly out to the little vessel, they quickly turned the tables on the Governor and his officials; and to their indignant surprise, Miller and his men found themselves prisoners in the hands of the rebels. Then the insurgents, with John Culpeper, now the acknowledged leader of the revolt, at their head, rowed ashore to the landing with their captives; and in the old house at Enfield, on a bluff near the bank of the river—so goes our local tradition—the angry and astonished Governor was imprisoned.

Then the revolutionists proceeded to "Little River Poynte," probably the settlement which afterwards grew into the town of Nixonton, and seized Timothy Biggs, the surveyor and deputy collector of customs, who had been wringing the tobacco tax from the farmers. Then breaking open the chests and the locks, they found and took possession of Miller's commission as collector of customs and returned to Enfield, where they locked Biggs up with Miller in Captain Crawford's house.

For two weeks the deputy governor and the deputy collector were kept close prisoners at Enfield. The revolutionists in the meanwhile drew up a document known as "The Remonstrance of the Inhabitants of Pasquotank," in which they stated the grievances that had led them to take this high-handed manner of circumventing Miller and Biggs in their tyrannical proceedings. This "remonstrance" was sent to the precincts of Currituck, Perquimans and Chowan; and the planters, following the example of their neighbors in Pasquotank, rose in insurrection against the other collectors of the hated customs and export tax, and arrested and deposed the collectors.

At the end of a fortnight, the insurgents decided to take Miller and Biggs to George Durant's home in Durant's Neck. So the prisoners were taken on board one of the planter's vessels; and down the Pasquotank, into the sound, and a short distance up Little River, the rebels sailed, accompanied by several vessels filled with armed men. As they passed the "Carolina," that saucy little ship, which as Miller afterwards indignantly reported to the Lords Proprietors, "had in all these confusions rid with Jack Ensign Flag and Pennon flying," just off the shore from Enfield, saluted Culpeper, Durant and their companions by firing three of her guns.

Arrived at Durant's home, where some seventy prominent men of the colony had assembled, the revolutionists proceeded to establish a government of their own. John Jenkins was appointed governor, an assembly of eighteen men was elected, and a court convened before which Miller and Biggs were brought for trial on a charge of treason. But before the trial was ended, Governor Eastchurch, who had arrived in Virginia while these affairs were taking place, sent a proclamation to the insurgents commanding them to disperse and return to their homes. This the bold planters refused to do, and in further defiance of Eastchurch, the new officials sent an armed force to prevent his coming into the colony.

Eastchurch appealed to Virginia to help him establish his authority in Carolina; but while he was collecting forces for this purpose he fell ill and died. Durant, Culpeper, Byrd and their comrades were now masters in Albemarle.

The interrupted trials were never completed. Biggs managed to escape and made his way to England. Miller was kept a prisoner for two years in a little log cabin built for the purpose at the upper end of Pasquotank, near where the old brick house now stands. In two years' time Miller also contrived to escape, and found his way back to the mother country.

For ten years the Albemarle colony prospered under the wise and prudent management of the officers, whom the people had put in charge of affairs without leave or license from lord or king. But finally Culpeper and Durant decided of their own accord to give up their authority and restore the management of affairs to the Proprietors. An amicable settlement was arranged with these owners of Albemarle, who, realizing the wrongs the settlers had suffered at the hands of Miller and his associates, made no attempt to punish the leaders of the rebellion. John Harvey was quietly installed as temporary governor until Seth Sothel, one of the Proprietors, should come to take up the reins of government himself.

So at Enfield Farm, now the property of one of Pasquotank's most successful farmers and business men, Mr. Jeptha Winslow, began a disturbance which culminated a hundred years later in the Revolutionary War; and here, in embryo form, in 1677, was the beginning of our republic — "a government of the people, for the people, by the people."

CHAPTER IV

THE HECKLEFIELD FARM

Of the old Hecklefield house on Little River in Perquimans County, mentioned so often in the Colonial Records as the place of meeting for the Governor's Council, the General Court, and on one notable occasion, as the legislative hall of the Grand Assembly of Albemarle, not one stick or stone is left standing to-day. Only a few bricks where the great chimney once stood now remain, to suggest to the imagination the hospitable hearth around whose blazing logs the Governor and his colleagues, the Chief Justice and his associates, and the Speaker of the Assembly and his fellow representatives used to gather, when the old home was the scene of the public meetings of the Albemarle Colony.

The Hecklefield home was located on Durant's Neck on the plantation adjoining the tract of land purchased by George Durant from Kilcokonen, the great chief of the Yeopims. Though no one now living remembers the ancient building, yet the residents of Durant's Neck to-day, many of whom are the descendants of the early settlers in that region, confidently point out the site of Captain Hecklefield's house, and with one accord agree to its location, "about three hundred yards to the north of the main Durant's Neck road, at the foot of the late Calvin Humphries' Lane."

An old sycamore tree, whose great girth gives evidence of the centuries it has seen, stands by the side of the road at the entrance to the lane. Its mottled trunk and wide spreading branches are one of the landmarks of the region. And beneath its sheltering boughs, Durant and Catchmaid, Pricklove and Governor Drummond himself, who, tradition claims, was one of the residents of Durant's Neck, may often have met to talk over the affairs of the infant settlement. Governor Hyde and Chief Justice Gale have doubtless often hailed with relief the glistening white branches and broad green leaves of the old tree, whose outlines had grown familiar through many a journey to Hecklefield's home on business of state.

No description of the house is now extant. But that the building must have been, for those days, large and commodious, is evident from the fact that so often beneath its roof the leading men of the colony gathered to transact affairs of public interest. On no less than twenty occasions did executive, judicial and legislative officers assemble at Captain Hecklefield's to perform their various duties. That a private home was chosen as the scene of these gatherings arose from the fact that for over forty years after the first recorded settlement in North Carolina, no town had been founded within her borders. Therefore no public building of any kind, court-house or capitol, had been erected, and the Council, the Assembly and the Court were held at the homes of those planters, whose houses were large enough to accommodate such assemblies.

Local tradition tells us that the first court ever held in our State was convened under a great beech still standing on Flatty Creek, an arm of the broad Pasquotank, in Pasquotank County. But no records of this court can be found, nor does tradition tell whether the judge and advocates, plaintiffs and defendants, witnesses and jury assembled beneath the branches of that ancient tree, still strong and sturdy, came in answer to the call for the Palatine Court, the General Court, or the more frequently assembled Precinct Court.

The first Albemarle Assembly in 1665, was also held out in the open, the verdant foliage of another historic tree for roof, the soft moss for carpet. But by 1670 the homes of the planters were being built of sufficient size to accommodate these public meetings; and from that time until Edenton was founded and became the seat of government, we find these private homes being used for public gatherings.

Of Captain John Hecklefield himself, though his name appears very frequently in the Colonial Records from 1702 until 1717, but little is known. Of his ancestry nothing can be ascertained, nor do we know how or when he came into Albemarle. It is not even certain that he owned the home assigned as his, for no record of lands bought by him can be found in the records of Perquimans County. But that he must have been a man of high social standing and of great weight in the community is evident from the fact that he was a deputy of the Lords Proprietors, and thus became ex officio one of the seven Associate Justices of the General Court. The fact also that his home was so often selected for the meeting of the General Court, a body which in colonial days corresponded very closely to our modern Supreme Court; that the Governor's Council of which he, as a deputy for one of the Lords, was a member, and, that on one occasion, the Albemarle Assembly was called to meet at his home, fixes his standing in the community.

The first mention made of Captain Hecklefield is found in Vol. I of the Colonial Records, where the following notice is inscribed: "At a General Court held at ye house of Captain John Hecklefield in Little River, Oct. 27, 1702. Being present the Hon. Samuel Swann, Esq., the Hon. William Glover, Esq., Jno. Hawkins, Esq."

From that day until 1717, we find many instances of these public gatherings at Captain Hecklefield's home. The most prominent men in the Albemarle Colony were often there assembled. To the sessions of the General Court came Edward Moseley, the Justice of the Court, leader of the Cary faction in the Glover-Cary disturbance of 1708, Chief Commissioner for North Carolina when the boundary line between Virginia and Carolina was established, Speaker of the Assembly for four years, master of plantations and many slaves, and withal a very courteous gentleman and learned scholar. Christopher Gale, first judicial officer in Carolina to receive the commission as Chief Justice, in wig and silken gown, upheld the majesty of the law at the sessions of the General Court, assisted by his confréres, John Porter, Thomas Symonds, and John Blount.

At the first Council held at Captain Hecklefield's, July 4, 1712, we find among the dignitaries assembled on that occasion, Edward Hyde, first Governor of North Carolina, as separate and distinct from South Carolina, and first cousin of Queen Anne. This lordly gentleman commanded "most awful respect," and doubtless received it from planter and farmer. With him came Thomas Pollock, leader of the Glover faction, owner of 55,000 acres of land, numerous flocks of sheep and herds of cattle and of many vessels trading with the New England and West Indian ports, a merchant prince of colonial days, and destined to become twice acting Governor of North Carolina.

Some years later, at a meeting of the Council in April, 1714, Charles Eden, lately appointed by the Proprietors to succeed Hyde, who had died of yellow fever during the trouble with the Tuscaroras, took the oath of office at Captain Hecklefield's home, and became Governor of North Carolina. Among the members of the Council present on this occasion were Colonel Thomas Byrd, Nathan Chevin, and William Reed, all prominent men in Pasquotank, and the two former, leading churchmen of that county, and active members of the vestry of St. John's Parish. Tobias Knight was also there, a wealthy resident of Bath then, though he too had formerly lived in Pasquotank. Knight was later to win notoriety as a friend and colleague of Teach, the pirate. And Governor Eden himself was later accused of collusion with Blackbeard, though no sufficient proof could be found to bring him to trial.

By what means of locomotion these high dignitaries of the colony found their way to Durant's Neck, we can only conjecture. Possibly a coach and four may have borne Governor Eden and Governor Hyde the long journey from Chowan and Bath to Hecklefield's door. Possibly Judge and advocate, members of the Assembly and councilors, preferred to make the trip on horseback, breaking the journey by frequent stops at the homes of the planters in the districts through which they traveled, meeting along the road friends and acquaintances bound on the same errand to the same destination. And as the cavalcade increased in numbers as it drew nearer the end of the journey, doubtless the hilarity of the travelers increased; and by the time the old sycamore was sighted, it was a gay, though weary, procession that turned into the lane and passed beneath its branches, down to where the old house stood near the banks of the river.

More probably, however, the members of Council, Court or Assembly, met at some wharf in their various precincts, and embarking on the swift sloops of the great planter, made the trip to Durant's Neck by water. Down the Pamlico, Chowan, Perquimans and Pasquotank the white-sailed vessels bore their passengers into Albemarle Sound and a short distance up Little River; then disembarking at the Hecklefield Landing, where the hospitable host of the occasion was doubtless waiting to receive the travelers, they made their way with many a friendly interchange of gossip and jest to the great house, standing back from the river beneath the arching branches of the sheltering sycamores.

One of the most interesting and important of all the public gatherings convened at the Hecklefield home was the meeting of the Assembly on October 11, 1708, to decide which of the two claimants of the office of President of the Council, or Deputy Governor of North Carolina, should have just right to that office. The two rival claimants were Thomas Cary, of the precinct of Pamlico, and William Glover, of Pasquotank. To understand the situation which necessitated the calling of a special session of the Assembly to settle the dispute between the two men, it may be well to review the events leading up to this meeting.

In 1704, when Queen Anne came to the throne of England, Parliament passed an act requiring all public officers to take an oath of allegiance to the new sovereign. The Quakers in Carolina, who in the early days of the colony were more numerous than any other religious body in Albemarle, had hitherto been exempt from taking an oath when they qualified for office. Holding religiously by the New Testament mandate, "Swear not at all," they claimed, and were allowed the privilege, of making a declaration of like tenor as the oath, substituting for the words, "I swear" the expression, to them equally binding, "I affirm."

But when Governor Henderson Walker died, Sir Nathaniel Johnson, then Governor of North and South Carolina, sent Major Robert Daniel from South Carolina to take Walker's place as Deputy Governor of the Northern Colony.

Daniel was an ardent member of the Church of England, and was strongly desirous of establishing this church in Carolina by law. But he knew that so long as the Quakers were members of the Assembly, and held high office in Albemarle, this law could never be passed. Therefore he determined to demand a strict oath of office from all who were elected to fill public positions. This determination was carried out. The Quakers were driven from the Assembly, which body, subservient to the new Governor, passed the law establishing the Church of England in Albemarle.

But the Quakers did not submit tamely to this deprivation of their ancient rights and privileges. Many of the most influential men in the colony, especially in Pasquotank and Perquimans, were Friends; and they determined to appeal to the Proprietors to uphold them in their claim to a share in the government. The Dissenters in the colony joined with them in their plea, and the result was that Governor Daniel was removed from office, and Governor Johnson ordered by the Lords to appoint another deputy for the Northern Colony. Thomas Cary, of South Carolina, received the appointment and came into Albemarle to take up the reins of government. But lo, and behold! no sooner was he installed in office than he, too, like Daniel, made it known that he would allow no one to hold office who refused to be sworn in, in the manner prescribed by Parliament.

Quakers and Dissenters again banded together, this time to have Cary deposed; and John Porter hastened to England to state their grievances to the Lords. Porter also petitioned in behalf of the Quakers and their supporters, that the law requiring the oaths should be set aside; and also that the colony should be allowed to choose its own Governor from its own Council.

The Lords again listened favorably to the petitioners, and Porter returned to Carolina, bringing with him a written agreement to the petition. Cary, during Porter's absence, had left the colony, and William Glover, of Pasquotank, was administering the government. On Porter's return, Glover was allowed to retain the office; but later, to the surprise and disappointment of Friend and Dissenter, he, too, decided to refuse to admit to office any who refused to take the hated oaths.

Cary returned at this juncture and demanded to be reinstated as Deputy Governor; and Porter and other former supporters of Glover now went to his side. A new Council was chosen, and Cary made its president, on condition, as we infer, that he carry out the will of the Proprietors as expressed in the commission given to Porter.

But Glover was by no means disposed to surrender his office tamely to Cary, and still claimed the authority with which he had been invested. Many prominent citizens supported him in his claim, Thomas Pollock, one of the most influential of the planters, being his warmest adherent. So now there were two governments in the colony, each claiming to be the only right and lawful one. Disputes over the matter grew so numerous and violent that finally the two factions agreed to leave the decision of the matter to a new Assembly which was elected at this juncture. And this was the Assembly that convened at Captain Hecklefield's in 1708.

Edward Moseley was elected Speaker; the rival claims of the two governors duly and hotly debated; and the result was, that Cary's friends being in the majority, that worthy was declared to be the true and lawful ruler of the colony. Glover, Pollock and Christopher Gale, disgusted with the turn affairs had taken, left Carolina and went to Virginia, where they remained for two years, at the end of which time Edward Hyde, the Queen's first cousin, was appointed Governor of North Carolina, and these malcontents returned to their homes in Albemarle.

And how did Madam Hecklefield manage to provide for the numerous guests who so often met around her fireside? The housewife to-day would rebel at such frequent invasions of the privacy of her home; and the high price of living would indeed prohibit such wholesale entertainment of the public; but in those good old days living was easy. The waters of Little River and Albemarle Sound teemed with fish; the woods were full of deer and other wild game; the fields were musical with the clear call of the quail; slaves were ready to do the bidding of the lady of the manor; wood was plentiful for the big fire-places, and candles easily moulded for the lighting of the rooms. No one in those days was used to the modern luxury of a private room and bath; and the guests doubtless shared in twos and threes and fours the rooms placed at their disposal. So, Madam Hecklefield, with a mind at ease from domestic cares, was able to greet her guests with unruffled brow.

The neighboring planters doubtless came to the rescue, and helped to provide bed and board for the gentry whom Captain Hecklefield could not accommodate; and the lesser fry found the humbler settlers on the "Neck" no less hospitable in opening their doors to them, though very probably good coin of the realm often settled the debt between guest and host.

After the meeting of the Assembly of 1708, various other public gatherings took place at the Hecklefield home, until November 22, 1717. On this occasion the colony was formally notified of the death of Queen Anne, and George I was proclaimed the "Liege Lord of Carolina."

At this meeting Governor Charles Eden was present, and serving with him were the Honorable Thomas Byrd, and Nathaniel Chevin, of Pasquotank, and Christopher Gale and Francis Foster, all deputies of the Proprietors.

This being the first recorded occasion in North Carolina of a proclamation announcing the death of one sovereign and ascension to the throne of another, the quaint phraseology of the original document may be of more interest than a modern version of its contents:

"Whereas we have received Certain Information from Virginia of the death of our late Sovereign Lady, Queen Anne, of Blessed Memory by whose death the Imperial Crownes of Greate Brittaine ffrance and Ireland are Solely and Rightfully Come to the High and Mighty Prince George Elector of Brunswick Luenburg—

"Wee therefore doe by this our proclamation with one full voice and Consent of Heart and Tongue Publish and proclaim that the High and Mighty Prince George Elector of Brunswick Luenburg is now by the death of our late Sovereigne of happy memory become our Lawful and rightful Leighe Lord George by the grace of God King of Greate Brittaine ffrance and Ireland, Defender of the Faith etc., To whom wee doe all hearty and humble affection. Beseeching Obedience with long and happy Years to raigne over us. Given etc., the 16th Day of November, 1714."

This proclamation having been duly read, the Governor and his Council proceeded to subscribe to the oath of allegiance to the new sovereign, as did Tobias Knight, collector of customs, from Currituck, and other public officers present.

This meeting, with one exception, a Council held in 1717, is the last recorded as occurring at the Hecklefield home. Edenton, founded in 1715, became the seat of government for a number of years, and meetings affecting the affairs of the colony were for the most part held there in the court-house built soon after.

Captain John Hecklefield's house on Little River now disappears from history; but though no longer the scene of the public activities of Albemarle, it doubtless kept up for many years its reputation as the center of all that was best in the social life of the colony.

CHAPTER V

COLONIAL DAYS IN CHURCH AND SCHOOL ON LITTLE RIVER, PASQUOTANK COUNTY

Among the many wide and beautiful rivers that drain the fertile lands of ancient Albemarle, none is more full of historic interest than the lovely stream known as Little River, the boundary set by nature to divide Pasquotank County on the east from her sister county, Perquimans, on the west.

On the shores of this stream, "little," as compared with the other rivers of Albemarle, but of noble proportions when contrasted with some of the so-called rivers of our western counties, the history of North Carolina as an organized government had its beginning.

As early as 1659 settlers began moving down into the Albemarle region from Virginia, among them being George Durant, who spent two years searching for a suitable spot to locate a plantation, finally deciding upon a fertile, pleasant land lying between Perquimans River on the west, and Little River on the east. Following Durant came George Catchmaid, John Harvey, John Battle, Dr. Thomas Relfe and other gentlemen, who settled on Pasquotank, Perquimans and Little rivers, buying their lands from the Indians; and later, when Charles II included the Albemarle region in the grant to the Lords Proprietors, taking out patents for their estates from these new owners of the soil, paying the usual quit-rents for the same.

John Jenkins, Valentine Byrd, and other wealthy men came later into this newly settled region, and by 1663 the Albemarle region was a settlement of importance, and Governor Berkeley, of Virginia, one of the Lords Proprietors, had, with the concurrence of his partners in this new land, sent William Drummond to govern the colony; and the Grand Assembly of Albemarle had held its first session at Hall's Creek, an arm of Little River, in Pasquotank County.

In 1664, when the Clarendon colony was broken up, many of the settlers from the Cape Fear region came into Albemarle; and in 1666 this section received a fresh influx of immigrants from the West Indies, many of whom settled upon Little River and embarked upon the then lucrative trade of ship-building. The usual natural advantages of the section made it in many respects a desirable land for the new comers. Still there were many drawbacks to the well being of the settlers, among the most serious of which was the lack of the two factors which make for the true progress of a country, educational and religious facilities and privileges.

Carolina was settled in a very different manner from most of her sisters among the thirteen colonies. To those regions settlers came in groups, often a whole community migrating to the new land, taking with them ministers, priests and teachers; and wherever they settled, however wild and desolate the land, they had with them those two mainstays of civilization.

But into the Albemarle colony the settlers came a family at a time; and instead of towns and town governments being organized, the well-to-do settlers with their families and servants established themselves upon large plantations, building their homes far apart, and devoting their time to agricultural pursuits.

So it is not surprising that for many years the only religious exercises in which the Carolina settler could take part were such as he held in his own home, the members of the Church of England reading the prayers and service of the Book of Common Prayer, the Dissenter using such service as appealed most to him.

As for the education of the children, the wealthy planter would often engage in his service some indentured servant, often a man of learning, who would gladly give his services for a number of years for the opportunity of coming to this new Land of Promise. And in later years as the boys of the family outgrew the home tutor, they were sent to the mother country to finish their education at Oxford or Cambridge.

But the poor colonist had none of these means of giving his children an education; and for many years, indeed, not until 1705, we can find no mention of any attempt on the part of the settlers to provide a school for the children of the poor.

But about twelve years after George Durant settled on Little River, the religious condition of Albemarle began to improve. In the spring of that year, William Edmundson, a faithful friend and follower of George Fox, the founder of the Quaker Church, came into

Albemarle and held the first public religious service ever heard in the colony at the house of Henry Phelps, who lived in Perquimans County, near where the old town of Hertford now stands. From there he went into Pasquotank, where he was gladly received and gratefully heard. The following fall George Fox came into the two counties himself, preached to the people and made a number of converts to the Quaker doctrine.

This religious body grew in numbers and influence, and according to the Colonial Records, "At a monthly meeting held at Caleb Bundy's house in 1703, it is agreed by Friends that a meeting-house be built at Pasquotank with as much speed as may be." And later, between 1703 and 1706, this plan was carried out, and on the banks of Symons Creek, an arm of Little River, between the two ancient settlements of Nixonton and Newbegun Creek, the first Quaker meeting-house (and with the exception of the old church in Chowan built by members of the Church of England), the first house of worship in the State, was built.

Rough and crude was this house of God, simple and plain the large majority of the men and women who gathered there to worship in their quiet, undemonstrative way the Power who had led them to this land of freedom. But the Word preached to these silent listeners in that rude building inspired within them those principles upon which the foundation of the best citizenship of our State was laid.

The Church of England, though long neglectful of her children in this distant colony, had by this time begun to waken to her duty towards the sheep of her fold in Carolina. Somewhere about 1700 a missionary society sent a clergyman to the settlement, and in 1708 the Rev. Mr. Ackers writes to Her Majesty's Secretary in London that "The Citizens of Pasquotank have agreed to build a church and two chapels." As to the location of these edifices, history remains silent; but that the church had been sowing good seed in this new and fertile soil is shown by the account given by the Rev. Mr. Adams of the people of Pasquotank, to whom he had been sent as rector of the parish in that county.

According to the letter written by Mr. Adams to Her Majesty's Secretary, there had come into the county with the settlers from the

West Indies a learned, public-spirited layman named Charles Griffin, who, seeing the crying need of the people, had established by 1705 a school on Symons Creek, for the children of the settlers near by.

Being a loyal son of the Church of England, he insisted upon reading the morning and evening service of that church daily in his school, and he required his young charges to join in the prayers and make the proper responses. So faithful and efficient a teacher did he prove that even the Quakers who had suffered many things from the Church of England, as well as from their dissenting brethren, were glad to send their children to his school.

The Colonial Records contain many references to the wide and beneficent influence exerted by Mr. Griffin while acting in his two-fold capacity of teacher and lay-reader in Pasquotank.

Governor Glover in a letter to the Bishop of London in 1708 writes: "In Pasquotank an orderly congregation has been kept together by the industry of a young gentleman whom the parish has employed to read the services of the Church of England. This gentleman being a man of unblemished life, by his decent behavior in that office, and by apt discourses from house to house, not only kept those he found, but gained many to the church."

Again and again in the pages of the Colonial Records, Vol. I, are the praises of Charles Griffin sung; though, sad to say, in the latter days of his life he seems to have fallen from grace, and to have become involved in some scandal, the particulars of which are not given. This scandal must have been proved unfounded, or he lived it down; for we hear of him in after years as a professor in William and Mary College.

History contains no record of the location of Charles Griffin's school, but according to tradition, and to the old inhabitants of that section, it was located on Symons Creek, not far from the ancient Quaker meeting-house. This latter building, erected somewhere between 1703 and 1706, was standing, within the memory of many among the older citizens of our county, some of whom retain vivid recollections of attending, when they were children, the services held by the Friends in this house of worship.

It may be of interest here to mention that the heirs of the late Elihu White, of Belvidere, to whom the property belonged, have lately donated the site of the meeting-house on Symons Creek to the Quakers of that section, of whom there are still quite a number. And once again, after a lapse of many years, will the ancient worship be resumed on the shores of that quiet stream.

To the pioneer settlers on Little River, then, belongs the honor of starting the wheels of government at Hall's Creek, of erecting on Symons Creek the second house of worship in the State, and of establishing on that same tributary of Little River the first school in North Carolina.

CHAPTER VI

THE HAUNTS OF BLACKBEARD

The name of the famous pirate, Teach, or Blackbeard, as he was familiarly known, plays a conspicuous part in the early history of North Carolina, and survives in many local traditions on our coast.

Many spots along our sounds and rivers have been honeycombed by diggers after the pirate's buried hoard. Tradition says that it was the gruesome custom of those fierce sea robbers to bury the murdered body of one of their own band beside the stolen gold, that his restless spirit might "walk" as the guardian of the spot. And weird tales are still told of treasure seekers who, searching the hidden riches of Teach and his band, on lonely islands and in tangled swamps along our eastern waterways, have been startled at their midnight task by strange sights and sounds, weird shapes and balls of fire, which sent the rash intruder fleeing in terror from the haunted spot.

Hardly a river that flows into our eastern sounds but claims to have once borne on its bosom the dreaded "Adventure," Blackbeard's pirate craft; hardly a settlement along those streams but retains traditions of the days when the black flag of that dreaded ship could be seen streaming in the breeze as the swift sails sped the pirates by, on murder and on plunder bent. Up Little River that flows by George Durant's home down to the broad waters of Albemarle Sound, Teach and his drunken crew would come, seeking refuge after some bold marauding expedition, in the hidden arms of that lovely stream. Up the beautiful Pasquotank, into the quiet waters of Symons Creek and Newbegun Creek, the dreaded bark would speed, and the settlers along those ancient streams would quake and tremble at the sound of the loud carousing, the curses and shouts that made hideous the night.

On all these waters "Teach's Light" is still said to shed a ghostly gleam on dark, winter nights; and where its rays are seen to rest, there, so the credulous believe, his red gold still hides, deep down in the waters or buried along the shore.

A few miles down the Pasquotank from Elizabeth City, North Carolina, there stands near the river shore a quaint old building known as "The Old Brick House," which is said to have been one of the many widely scattered haunts of Blackbeard. A small slab of granite, circular in shape, possibly an old mill wheel, is sunken in the ground at the foot of the steps and bears the date of 1709, and the initials "E.T."

The ends of the house are of mingled brick and stone, the main body of wood. The wide entrance hall, paneled to the ceiling, opens into a large room, also paneled, in which is a wide fire-place with a richly carved mantel reaching to the ceiling. On each side of this mantel there is a closet let into the wall, one of which communicates by a secret door with the large basement room below. Tradition says that from this room a secret passage led to the river; that here the pirate confined his captives, and that certain ineffaceable stains upon the floor in the room above, hint of dark deeds, whose secret was known only to the underground tunnel and the unrevealing waters below.

Standing on a low cliff overlooking the Pasquotank, whose amber waters come winding down from the great Dismal Swamp some ten miles away, the old house commands a good view of the river, which makes a wide bend just where the ancient edifice stands. And a better spot the pirate could not have found to keep a lookout for the avenging ship that should track him to his hiding place. And should a strange sail heave in sight, or one which he might have cause to fear was bringing an enemy to his door, quickly to the secret closet near the great mantel in the banquet hall would Blackbeard slip, drop quietly down to the basement room beneath, bending low, rush swiftly through the underground tunnel, slip into the waiting sloop and be off and away up the river or down, whichever was safest, out of reach of the enemy.

But though many of the streams and towns in the Albemarle region retain these traditions of Blackbeard, in little Bath, the oldest town in North Carolina, can the greatest number of these tales be heard; and with good reason, for here in this historic village, the freebooter made his home for a month or so after he had availed himself of the king's offer of pardon to the pirates who would surrender themselves and promise to give over their evil mode of life.

This ancient village, founded in 1705, is situated on Bath Creek, by which modest name the broad, beautiful body of water, beside which those early settlers built their homes, is called. The banks of the creek are high and thickly wooded, rising boldly from the water, in striking contrast with the low, marshy shores of most of our eastern rivers.

Near the shores of the creek, just outside the town, there is still to be seen a round brick structure resembling a huge oven, called Teach's Kettle, in which the pirate is said to have boiled the tar with which to calk his vessels. Across the creek from the town are the ruins of "the Governor's Mansion," where, it is claimed, Governor Eden died. In an old field a short distance from the mansion is a deep depression filled with broken bricks, which was the governor's wine cellar. Nearly on a line with this, at the water's edge, is shown the opening of a brick tunnel, through which the Pirate Teach is said to have conveyed his stolen goods into the governor's wine cellar for safe keeping. That Governor Eden, for reasons best known to himself, winked at the pirate's freebooting expeditions, and that there was undoubtedly some collusion between Blackbeard and the chief magistrate of the State, was generally believed; though Eden vehemently denied all partnership with the freebooter.

To the latter class of narrative the following thrilling tale, which combines very ingeniously the various points of historic interest in Bath, must, it is to be feared, belong. The story goes that Blackbeard, with the consent of her father, was suing for the hand of Governor Eden's daughter. The young lady, for the excellent reason that she preferred another and better man, declined absolutely to become the pirate's bride.

Finally, in a desperate attempt to elude his pursuit, Miss Eden bribed two of her father's slaves to row her across the creek in the dead of the night to Bath. Here she took refuge in the "Old Marsh House" with her friend, Mrs. Palmer, whose memorial tablet is now in St. Thomas Church at Bath, the oldest house of worship in the State.

Teach, infuriated at the lady's continued rejection of his suit, put out to sea on one of his piratical excursions. The prize he captured on this occasion was Miss Eden's lover, his hated rival. The story goes that Blackbeard cut off one of the hands of the unfortunate captive, threw his body into the sea, and enclosing the gruesome relic in a silver casket, as if it were some costly gift, sent it with many compliments to his lady love. When the unfortunate maiden opened the casket and saw the ghastly object she uttered a terrible shriek and swooned from horror; then, as was the fashion in the old romances, pined slowly away and died of a broken heart.

Now, at first blush, it seems that this interesting tale has enough corroborating evidences of its veracity to pass down to the coming ages as true history. A visitor to Bath can see for himself every one of the places mentioned in the story. The tablet in old St. Thomas Church testifies in many a high-sounding phrase the many virtues of Miss Eden's friend, Mrs. Margaret Palmer; and the "Old Marsh House" is still standing, a well preserved and fascinating relic of the past, where the above lady is said to have sheltered her friend. We speak of facts as hard and stubborn things, but dates are as the nether millstone for hardness. And here are the rocks on which our lovely story shatters: Teach was captured and beheaded in 1718; Mrs. Palmer's tablet reports her to have been born in 1721, and the Marsh House was not built until 1744. The story is a beautiful instance of the way in which legends are made.

After so much that is traditional, a brief sketch of the pirate's life may not be amiss. According to Francis Xavier Martin's History of North Carolina, Edward Teach was born in Bristol, England. While quite young he took service on a privateer and fought many years for king and country with great boldness. In 1796 he joined one Horngold, one of a band of pirates who had their rendezvous in the Bahamas, taking refuge when pursued, in the sounds and rivers of North Carolina.

On his first cruise with the pirate, Teach captured a sloop, of which Horngold gave him the command. He put forty guns on board, named the vessel "Queen Anne's Revenge," and started on a voyage to South America. Here Teach received news of the king's proclamation of pardon for all pirates who would surrender themselves. So, having collected much plunder, and wishing to secure it, he came to North Carolina. With twenty of his men he proceeded to Governor Eden's house, surrendered himself and received the king's pardon.

Soon after, Blackbeard married a young girl, his thirteenth wife, and settled down near Bath with the intention, apparently, of becoming a peaceable citizen; but his good resolutions were soon broken; "being good" did not appeal to the bold sea rover, and soon he was back again on the high seas, pursuing unchecked his career of plunder.

Finally, the people in desperation, finding Governor Eden either unable or unwilling to put an end to the pirate's depredations, appealed to Governor Spotswood, of Virginia, for aid, and the pirate was finally captured and beheaded by Lieutenant Maynard, whom Spotswood put in command of the ship that went out to search for this terror of the seas.

Seen through the softening haze of two centuries, the figure of the redoubtable sea robber acquires a romantic interest, and it is not surprising that many good and highly respected citizens of eastern North Carolina number themselves quite complacently among the descendants of the bold buccaneer.

CHAPTER VII

THE OLD BRICK HOUSE—A TRUE HISTORY OF THE HISTORIC DWELLING REPUTED TO BE THE HOME OF THE FAMOUS PIRATE

Local tradition claims that the old brick house described in the foregoing chapter, was once a haunt of the famous pirate, Edward Teach, or Blackbeard, as he was commonly called.

Wild legends of lawless revel and secret crime have grown up about the old building, until its time-stained walls seem steeped in the atmosphere of gloom and terror which the poet Hood has so graphically caught in his "Haunted House":

> "But over all there hung
> a cloud of fear—
> A sense of mystery, the
> spirit daunted,
> And said as plain as
> whisper in the ear,
> 'The house is haunted.'"

It is said that the basement room of the Brick House served as a dungeon for prisoners taken in Teach's private raids and held for ransom.

There are darker stories, too, of deeds whose secret was known only to the hidden tunnel and unrevealing waters below.

But tradition has been busy with other occupants of the old house. It is said to have been in colonial days the home of a branch of an ancient and noble English family.

"THE OLD BRICK HOUSE," ON PASQUOTANK RIVER

To the care of these gentlefolk their kinsmen of old England were said to have entrusted a young and lovely girl in order to separate her from a lover, whose fortunes failed to satisfy the ambition of her proud and wealthy parents.

The lover followed his fair one across the seas, and entered in disguise among the guests assembled at the great ball which was given at the Brick House in honor of their recently arrived and charming guest. The young lady's brother, who had accompanied her to this country, penetrated the disguise of her lover.

"Words of high disdain and insult" passed between the young men, a duel followed, and the lover fell, leaving on the floor dark stains which are said to remain to this day, in silent witness to the tragedy of long ago.

Many years after, in a closet of the old house, a faded pink satin slipper was found which tradition naturally assigns to the fair but unhappy heroine of the old tale of love and death.

So much for tradition.

The story of Teach's occupation of the Old Brick House has not been received without question, but in default of more accurate knowledge, it has been accepted.

Recently, certain facts have come to light concerning the ancient building which are briefly given below.

The information referred to was given by Mr. Joseph Sitterson, a prominent resident of Williamston, North Carolina.

According to Mr. Sitterson, the Old Brick House was the property of his great grandmother, Nancy Murden. This lady was a descendant of Lord Murden, who in 1735 sent out an expedition in charge of his eldest son to make a settlement in the New World.

The party obtained, whether by grant or purchase is not known, the land on which the Old Brick House now stands. A sandy ridge extends into Camden County, and is known to this day as Murden's Ridge.

Young Murden had brought with him from England the brick and stone, the carved mantel and paneling, which entered into the construction of the new home he now proceeded to build.

It is thought that the house was intended to be entirely of brick; but the end walls of the massive chimneys having exhausted the supply, the building was finished with wood. The house was planned with the greatest care for defense against the Indian raids; hence the sliding panels, and the roomy and secret spaces in which the family plate and jewels brought from the old country could be quickly concealed, in case of sudden attack.

With the same end in view, there were built in the basement, from the rich timber of the adjoining woods, stalls of cedar, the narrow windows of which can still be seen. In these stalls the ponies were kept for fear of Indian raids.

It is believed that in the troubled times preceding the American Revolution, Lord Murden's son succeeded to his father's large estates and returned to England to claim his inheritance.

After the Revolution, his American lands were confiscated and became the property of the State.

Shortly after the war two brothers of the Murden family came to North Carolina, entered the old property and took charge of it.

These brothers married sisters, the Misses Sawyer. In time the Old Brick House came into the possession of Nancy Murden, a descendant of one of the brothers Murden.

At her death she left the property as follows: One-third to Isaac Murden, one-third to Jerry Murden, one-third to Nancy Murden, her grandchildren.

This will is recorded in the court-house at Elizabeth City, North Carolina.

CHAPTER VIII

"ELMWOOD," THE OLD SWANN HOMESTEAD IN PASQUOTANK COUNTY

On a low bluff, overlooking the waters of the beautiful Pasquotank River, some five or six miles from Elizabeth City, there stood until a few years before the outbreak of the Civil War, an old colonial mansion known as "Elmwood," the home for many years of the historic Swann family, who were among the earliest settlers in our State, and played a prominent part in the colonial history of North Carolina.

Mrs. J.P. Overman, of Elizabeth City, whose father, the late Dr. William Pool, of Pasquotank County, spent his boyhood days at Elmwood, then the home of his father, has given the writer a description of this historic house, as learned from her father: "The house was situated on the right-hand bank of the river, and was set some distance back from the road. It was built of brick brought from England, and was a large, handsome building for those days. As I recall my father's description of it, the house was two stories high; a spacious hall ran the full length of the house, both up-stairs and down; and in both the upper and lower story there were two large rooms on each side of the hall. A broad, massive stairway led from the lower hall to the one above. The house stood high from the ground, the porch was small for the size of the building, and the windows were high and narrow. The ceilings of the rooms on the first floor had heavy, carved beams of cedar that ran the length of the house. On the left of the house as you approached from the river road, stretched a dense woods, abounding in deer, and in those days these animals would venture near the homes of men, and feed in the fields."

The great planters in those early days in North Carolina, spent their working hours looking after the affairs of their estates, settling the disputes of their tenants, and attending with their fellow-landed neighbors the sessions of the General Assembly, and of the courts. Their pleasures were much the same as those of their kinsmen across the sea in merry England—fox-hunting, feasting and dancing; though to these amusements of the old country were added the more exciting deer chase, and the far more dangerous pastime of a bear hunt, when bruin's presence near the homestead became too evident for comfort. Often the wild screams of the fierce American panther would call the planters forth into the dark forests at their doors, and then it must be a hunt to the death, for until that cry was stilled, every house within the shadow of the forest was endangered. Among the homes of the planters in the ancient counties of Pasquotank, Currituck, Perquimans and Chowan, Elmwood was noted for the hospitality of its earliest owners, the Swanns; and the long list of prominent families who afterwards lived within its walls, kept alive the old traditions of hospitality.

On many a clear, crisp autumn day, the lawn in front of the mansion would be filled with gentry on horseback, dressed after the fashion of their "neighbors" across the sea in hunting coats of pink, ready for a hunt after the wily fox. The master of the hounds, William Swann himself, would give the signal for the eager creatures to be unloosed, the bugle would sound, and the cry "off and away" echo over the fields, and the chase would be on. A pretty run would reynard give his pursuers, and often the shades of evening would be falling ere the hunters would return to Elmwood, a tired, bedraggled and hungry group. Then at the hospitable board the day's adventures would be related, and after the dinner a merry dance would close the day.

At Christmas, invitations would be issued to the families of the gentry in the nearest counties, to attend a great ball at Elmwood. The old house would be filled from garret to cellar, and the hospitable homes of nearby friends would open to take in the overflow of guests. Dames and maidens coy, clad in the quaint and picturesque colonial costume, with powdered hair and patches, in richly brocaded gowns and satin slippers, made stately courtesy to gay dandies and jovial squires arrayed in coats of many colors, broidered vests, knee breeches and silken hose, brilliant buckles at knee and on slippers, their long hair worn ringleted and curled, or tied in queues. In stately measure the graceful minuet would open the ball. Then the gayer strains of the old Virginia reel would cause even the dignified dame or sober squire to relax; and in laughter and merrymaking the hours would speed, till the gradual paling of the stars and a flush in the east would warn the merry dancers that "the night was far spent, and the day was at hand."

Such are the tales still told in our county of the olden days at Elmwood — tales handed down from father to son, and preserved in the memories of the old inhabitants of Pasquotank. And all such memories should be preserved and recorded ere those who hold them dear have passed away, and with them, the traditions that picture to a generation all too heedless of the past, the life of these, our pioneer forefathers.

From this old home more distinguished men have gone forth than probably from any other home in North Carolina.

The Hon. J. Bryan Grimes in an address made before the State Historical Society at Raleigh in 1909, gives a long list of eminent Carolinians who have called Elmwood their home. Among them were Colonel Thomas Swann and Colonel William Swann, both in colonial days Speakers of the Assembly; three members of the family by the name of Samuel Swann, and John Swann, members of Congress. Here lived Fred Blount, son of Colonel John Blount, an intimate friend of Governor Tryon. William Shephard, a prominent Federalist, for some years made Elmwood his home. The Rev. Solomon Pool, President of the University of North Carolina, and his brother, John Pool, United States Senator from North Carolina, both spent their boyhood days in this ancient mansion. And, as Colonel Grimes' researches into the history of this old home have made known, and as he relates in his speech on "The Importance of Memorials," "At Elmwood lived, and with it were identified, ten Speakers of the Assembly, five Congressmen, one United States Senator, one President of the State University, and one candidate for Governor."

One of the Samuel Swanns who resided at Elmwood was the brave young surveyor, who, with his comrades, Irvine and Mayo, was the first to plunge into the tangled depths of the Dismal Swamp, when the boundary line between North Carolina and Virginia was established.

Before the War between the States had been declared, the old house was burned to the ground; and since then the estate has been cut into smaller farms, and the family burying-ground has been desecrated by treasure-seekers, who in their mad greed for gold have not hesitated to disturb the bones of the sacred dead.

Just when or how the old home was burned, no one is able to tell. Whatever the circumstances of the destruction of this fine old building, the loss sustained by the county, and by the State, is irreparable.

CHAPTER IX

PASQUOTANK IN COLONIAL WARS

The earliest wars in which the pioneers of North Carolina took part were those fought between the first comers into the State and the Indians. As Pasquotank was one of the earliest of the counties to be settled, we might naturally expect that county to have taken an active part in those encounters. The fact, however, that the great majority of her early settlers were Friends, or Quakers, as they are more commonly called, prevented Pasquotank from sharing as extensively as she otherwise might have done in the fight for existence that the pioneers in Carolina were compelled to maintain; for one of the most rigid rules of the Quaker Church is that its members must not take up arms against their fellow men, no matter what the provocation may be.

However, a search through the Colonial Records reveals the fact that our county has given a fair quota of men and money whenever the domestic or foreign troubles of colony, state or nation, needed her aid.

The first encounter between our sturdy Anglo-Saxon forefathers and the red man of the forest occurred in 1666, two years after William Drummond took up the reins of government in Albemarle. After this trouble little is recorded, nor is Pasquotank nor any of her precincts mentioned in reference to the Indian War. But as the majority of the settlers in North Carolina then lived along the shores of Little River and the Pasquotank, we may feel sure that the men of this county were prominent in subduing their savage foes, who, as Captain Ashe records, "were so speedily conquered that the war left no mark upon the infant settlement."

From then until the terrible days of the Tuscarora Massacre of 1711, the county, and Albemarle as a whole, rested from serious warfare; but these years can hardly be termed peaceful ones for the settlers in this region. The Culpeper Rebellion, the dissatisfaction caused by the tyrannical and illicit deeds of Seth Sothel, the disturbance caused by Captain Bibbs, who claimed the office of governor in defiance of Ludwell, whom the Lords had appointed to rule over

Carolina, and the Cary troubles, all combined to keep the whole Albemarle district in a state of confusion and disorder for many years.

But all of these quarrelings and brawlings were hushed and forgotten when in September, 1711, the awful tragedy of the Tuscarora Massacre occurred. Though the settlers south of Albemarle Sound, in the vicinity of Bath and New Bern, and on Roanoke Island, suffered most during those days of horror, yet from the letters of the Rev. Rainsford and of Colonel Pollock, written during these anxious days, we learn that the planters north of the sound came in for their share of the horrors of an Indian uprising that swept away a large proportion of the inhabitants of the colony, and left the southern counties almost depopulated.

Though nearly paralyzed by the blow that had fallen upon the colony, which, in spite of difficulties, had been steadily growing and prospering, the officers of the government as soon as possible began to take steps to punish the Tuscaroras and their allies for the unspeakable atrocities committed by them during the awful days of the massacre, and also to devise means for conquering the savage foes who were still pursuing their bloody work. All the able-bodied men in the State were called upon to take part in the warfare against the Indians. But so few were left alive to carry on the struggle, that Governor Hyde was compelled to call upon the Governor of South Carolina and of Virginia to come to his aid in saving the colony from utter extinction. South Carolina responded nobly and generously. Virginia, for various reasons, sent but little aid to her afflicted sister colony. For two long years the war continued, until at last the Indians were conquered, the surviving hostile Tuscaroras left the State, and peace was restored to the impoverished and sorely tried colony.

During the bloody struggle, Pasquotank, which, with the other northern counties suffered but little in comparison with the counties south of the Albemarle, had sent what help she could to those upon whom the horrors of the war had fallen most heavily. In the Colonial Records this entry of services rendered by Pasquotank is found in a letter sent by Lieutenant Woodhouse and Thomas Johnson to certain "Gentlemen, Friends, and Neighbors," dated October 3, 1712.

"Captain Norton, as I was informed by Mrs. Knight, sailed last week from Pasquotank in Major Reed's sloop, with 30 or 40 men, provisions, and two barrels of gunpowder and ten barrels, I think, of shot." The destination of ship, men and cargo was Bath, the scene of the most disastrous of the Indian outbreaks.

In an extract from a "Book of the Orders and Judgments and Decrees of the Hon. Edward Hyde, Esq., President of the Council," mentioned in Dr. Hawk's History of North Carolina, we find the following entry: "Ordered that Capt. Edward Allard shall depart with his sloop "Core Sound Merchant" to Pasquotank River, and there take from on board the "Return," Mr. Charles Worth Glover, so much corn as will load his sloop, give to Mr. Glover a receipt for the same, and that he embrace the first fair wind and weather to go to Bath County and there apply himself to the Hon. John Barnewell, Esq., and follow such instructions as he shall receive from him."

Again, in a letter from the Rev. Giles Rainsforth to "Jno. Chamberlain, Esq.," written from "Chowan in North Carolina July 25, 1712," further mention is made of Pasquotank's part in the Tuscarora War: "Col. Boyde was the other day sent out with a party against the Indians, but was unfortunately shot through the head and few of his men came home, but shared his fate and fell sacrifices to the same common misfortune."

It has been charged against Pasquotank that her citizens did not respond to the call for volunteers to take part in the Tuscarora War; and it is true that the Quakers in the county did enjoin upon their brethren that they should not bear arms in this or any other disturbance. It is also true that a number of the citizens in the county did obey this injunction; and when the war was over we find that certain members of the Friends' meeting were brought to trial by the courts "for not going out in ye Indian Wars." But enough instances have been recorded to show that our county did take an active part in breaking the power of the Tuscaroras and in driving them from the State.

In 1715, when South Carolina in her turn underwent the horrors of an Indian war, and appealed to North Carolina for aid, we find that men from Pasquotank joined with other forces from the colony in response to this appeal. Captain John Pailin and Captain John

Norton, both of Pasquotank, are ordered "to draw out their companies and go to the assistance of South Carolina in the Yamassie War." And furthermore the command reads: "If men refuse, each captain is ordered to draft ten men who have small families or none, and to put them under Captain Hastins." That drafting was not resorted to, and that the men went willingly to the aid of their brethren in South Carolina, who rendered the northern colony such generous assistance in the Tuscarora War, is proved by the fact that fifty men were raised by the two captains, and cheerfully marched to the front along with the bands of militia from the neighboring counties.

So in these earliest trials of the military courage of her citizens, the county proved that she could and would take a worthy part.

CHAPTER X

PASQUOTANK IN COLONIAL WARS — "THE WAR OF JENKINS' EAR"

After the war with the Tuscaroras was over, and most of that powerful tribe had left the State, going to New York and becoming the sixth of the tribes there called "The Six Nations," for many years there were no pitched battles between the red men and the settlers in North Carolina.

But the troubles with the Indians did not end with the Tuscarora War; for though a treaty was made in 1713 with Tom Blount, king of the Tuscaroras, who remained in the State, whereby the Indians bound themselves to keep the peace, yet, as late as 1718 the colonists were still putting troops in the field to "catch or kill the enemy Indians." Indeed the settlers in Albemarle suffered as much from the Indians after the Tuscaroras left the State as they did during the days of the Indian massacre of 1711, and of the open warfare that followed.

In 1714 another Indian outbreak occurred, and the alarm was so great that many of the settlers in the Albemarle region determined to flee to Virginia, where the government seemed better able to protect its citizens than were the officials of North Carolina.

To prevent such an immigration from the colony, Governor Eden, who had succeeded Edward Hyde, issued a proclamation forbidding the people to leave the colony; and Governor Spotswood, of Virginia, gave orders to arrest any Carolinians who should flee into his colony without a passport from duly authorized officials in Carolina.

But as the years passed on, the Indian troubles gradually ceased, and the red men mostly disappeared from the eastern portion of the State, though as late as 1731 Dr. Brickwell speaks of finding there "a nation called the Pasquotanks, who kept cattle and made butter, but at present have not cattle."

With the dangers from the Indians over, and with the transfer of Carolina from the hands of the neglectful Lords Proprietors into the possession of King George II, brighter and more prosperous days began to dawn for North Carolina. The population rapidly increased; and, whereas, in 1717 there were only 2,000 persons in the colony, by 1735 this number had increased to 4,000. Lively wranglings there were often between the Royal Governors and the sturdy and independent members of the Grand Assembly, who resolutely carried out their purpose to preserve the constitutional rights of the people of the province. But no war cloud darkened the skies for many years after the Indian troubles were over.

Not until 1740 was there again a call to arms heard in North Carolina; then trouble arose between Spain and England, and the colonists in America were called upon to aid their Sovereign, King George II, in his war against the haughty Don.

The real cause of this war was the constant violation on the part of the English of the commercial laws which Spain had made to exclude foreign nations from the trade of her American colonies. But the event which precipitated matters and gave to the conflict which followed the name of "The War of Jenkins' Ear," was as follows:

The Spanish captured an English merchant vessel, whose master they accused of violating the trade laws of Spain. In order to wring a confession from the master, Captain Jenkins, his captors hung him up to the yard arms of his ship until he was nearly dead, and then let him down, thinking he would confess. But on his stoutly denying that he had been engaged in any nefarious dealings, and since no proof could be found against him, the captain of the Spanish ship cut off one of the English captain's ears, and insolently told him to show it to his countrymen as a warning of what Englishmen might expect who were caught trading with Spain's colonies in America.

Captain Jenkins put the ear in his pocket, sailed home as fast as wind and wave would carry him, and was taken straight to the House of Parliament with his story. Such was the indignation of both Lords and Commons at this insult to one of their nation, and so loud was the clamor for vengeance, that even Walpole, who for years had managed to hold the English dogs of war in leash, was now compelled to yield to the will of the people, and Parliament declared war with Spain.

Immediately upon this declaration, King George called upon his "trusty and well beloved subjects in Carolina" and the other twelve colonies, to raise troops to help the mother country in her struggle with arrogant Spain. Carolina responded nobly to the call for troops, as the following extract from a letter from Governor Gabriel Johnston to the Duke of Newcastle will testify: "I can now assure your grace that we have raised 400 men in this province who are just going to put to sea. In those Northern Parts of the Colony adjoining to Virginia, we have got 100 men each, though some few deserted since they began to send them on board the transports at Cape Fear. I have good reason to believe we could have raised 200 more if it had been possible to negotiate the Bills of Exchange in this part of the Continent; but as that was impossible we were obliged to rest satisfied with four companies. I must in justice to the assembly of the Province inform Your Grace that they were very zealous and unanimous in promoting this service. They have raised a subsidy of 1200 pounds as it is reckoned hereby on which the men have subsisted ever since August, and all the Transports are victualed."

While no mention is made of Pasquotank in this war, nor of men from any other county save New Hanover, we may reasonably infer that among the three hundred troops from the northern counties adjoining Virginia, men from our own county were included. No record has been kept of the names of the privates who enlisted from Carolina in this war. Nor do we know how many of those who at the king's call left home and country to fight a foreign land ever returned to their native shores; but we do know that these Carolina troops took part in the disastrous engagements of Cartagena and Boca-Chica; and that King George's troops saw fulfilled Walpole's prophecy made at the time of the rejoicing over the news that Parliament had declared war with Spain: "You are ringing the joy bells now," said the great Prime Minister, "but before this war is over you will all be wringing your hands!"

After the two crushing defeats of Cartagena and Boca-Chica, the troops from the colonies who still survived embarked upon their ships to return home; but while homeward bound a malignant fever broke out among the soldiers which destroyed nine out of every ten men on the ships. But few of those from Carolina lived to see their native home again. That they bore themselves bravely on the field of battle, none who know the war record of North Carolina will dare deny; though as regards her private soldiers in this war, history is silent.

One of the officers from Carolina, Captain Innes, of Wilmington, made such a record for gallantry during the two engagements mentioned, that in the French and Indian War, in which fourteen years later, not only the Thirteen Colonies, but most of the countries of Europe as well, were embroiled, he was made commander-in-chief of all the American forces, George Washington himself gladly serving under this distinguished Carolinian.

CHAPTER XI

A SOLDIER OF THE REVOLUTION — THE STORY OF A PASQUOTANK BOY WHO FOLLOWED WASHINGTON

It is a well known fact that the records of the services of the North Carolina soldiers who took part in the Revolutionary War are very meagre. Of the private, and other officers of leaser rank, this is especially true. Therefore, it is not surprising that a search through the Colonial Records for a statement of the services rendered his country by John Koen, a brave soldier of the Revolution from Pasquotank County, reveals only this fact: that he enlisted in Moore's Company, Tenth Regiment, on May 30, 1777, and served for three years.

But in addition to the above information, the following incidents in the life of John Koen have been furnished the writer of this history by Mrs. Margaret Temple, formerly of Rosedale, now a resident of Elizabeth City.

Mrs. Temple is a granddaughter of Colonel Koen, the widow of William S. Temple, a brave Confederate soldier from Pasquotank, and the mother of two of our former townsmen, Hon. Oscar Temple, of Denver, Colorado, and Robert Temple, of New Orleans.

Mrs. Temple was about twelve years old at the time of Colonel Koen's death, and retains a very vivid recollection of the stirring stories of the Revolution told by her grandfather during the long winter evenings, when the family gathered around the big fire-place in the old Koen homestead near Rosedale.

A record copied from the Koen family Bible states that John Koen, son of Daniel Koen and Grace Koen, his wife, was born on the 27th day of January, 1759; and years later this record was entered: "John Koen, departed this life September 5th, 1840, aged 83 yrs."

At the age of eighteen he entered his country's service as a volunteer, and served through the Revolution, participating in many of the greatest victories won by the Americans, sharing the worst hardships of the war with his fellow patriots, and laying down his arms only after Cornwallis had surrendered his sword at Yorktown.

At the beginning of the winter of 1775-1776, North Carolina was confronting the most perilous conditions which she had ever been called to face. From the north, east and west, the foe was pressing, while within her own borders the Tories were rising, and planning to join the British in the subjection of this rebellious state.

The plan formulated by the enemy was this: Sir Henry Clinton, with troops of British regulars, was to come down the coast to the mouth of the Cape Fear River, where Lord Cornwallis, who with seven regiments from England was hastening across the Atlantic, was to join him. Lord Dunmore, Royal Governor of Virginia, was to incite the slaves and indentured servants in the Albemarle district to unite with the Tories in the State; and the Indians in the western counties were to be induced to take up arms against the whites.

If these plans had matured, North Carolina would have been overpowered, but one by one they were frustrated. The battle of Great Bridge defeated Dunmore in his purpose. The Snow Campaign quieted the Indian uprising. The battle of Moore's Creek Bridge crashed the Tories, and the heavy winter storms delayed Cornwallis and prevented him from joining Clinton at the mouth of the Cape Fear.

When Lord Dunmore issued his proclamation offering freedom to the slaves and indentured servants who should join his majesty's forces, and then followed up this notice by burning and ravaging the plantations around Norfolk, Virginia, called upon her sister State for help, and Long and Sumner, from Halifax, and Warren, Skinner and Daugé from Perquimans and Pasquotank counties, hastened with their minute men and volunteers to Great Bridge, where Colonel Woodford in command of the Virginia troops, had thrown up fortifications.

Among the volunteers who were hastening to the scene of action was John Koen, of Pasquotank, a boy in years, but a man in purpose and resolution.

On December 9, 1775, the British attacked the fortifications, and the sound of heavy firing at Great Bridge, the first battle in which the men of the Albemarle section had been called to participate, was heard by the dwellers in the counties nearest Norfolk.

The story is still told by old residents of Rosedale, that John Koen's mother, who was washing the breakfast dishes when the firing began, hearing the first heavy reverberations from the cannon some thirty miles away, dropped the dish she was wiping, and in her motherly anxiety for the safety of her boy, cried out, "Dodge, John, dodge!"

Whether John dodged or not we do not know, but we do know that he bore his part manfully in this, his first battle, and shared in the victory which drove Dunmore from Virginia, and saved North Carolina from invasion from that direction, and a threatened uprising of the slaves.

On February 26, 1776, the battle of Moore's Creek Bridge was fought, which defeated the Tories in Carolina, and convinced the British that further attempts at this time to conquer the State were useless. So, toward the end of May, Clinton's fleet sailed from the mouth of Cape Fear River to Charleston, South Carolina, where his intention was to reduce that city.

Generals Charles Lee and Robert Howe, of the Continental army, hastened immediately to the defense of that city, and among the soldiers who followed them was John Koen. Here again the British were defeated, Colonel Moultrie's Palmetto fortifications proving an effective defense to the city by the sea, and Thompson's South Carolinians and North Carolinians bravely repelling the British land troops. Here Koen fought by the side of the soldiers of North Carolina, and here, possibly, he was an eye witness of the brave deed by which Sergeant Jasper won undying fame.

The British fleet, repulsed in the attempt to capture Charleston, sailed northward, the danger of invasion that for six months threatened the South was over, and we find many of the soldiers in North Carolina released from duty and returning to their homes.

But John Koen's heart was filled with boyish love and admiration for the commander-in-chief of the American army, and his one desire now was to follow Washington; so, shouldering his musket, the hardy young soldier marched away to offer his services to the great general.

We do not know whether or not John Koen was with Washington in the battle at Long Island and at White Plains, but from his own account as related by him to his family, he did have the glorious honor of sharing in the victory at Trenton on December 26, 1776.

Most of us are familiar with the picture of "Washington Crossing the Delaware," wherein he is represented standing erect in a small boat that seems about to be dashed to pieces by the heavy waves and the cakes of ice, but according to Colonel Koen, who was with Washington on that momentous night, no boats were used. The river was frozen over, and the soldiers, in order to keep their footing on the slippery ice, laid their muskets down on the frozen river and walked across on them to the Jersey shore. At times the ice bent so beneath the tread of the men that they momentarily expected to be submerged in the dark waters, but the dangerous crossing was safely made, the British and Hessian troops, spending the holiday hours in feasting and carousing at Trenton, were captured, and a great victory won for the American army.

Some time in the spring of 1777, John Koen must have returned to his home in Pasquotank County, for we find in the Colonial Records that in the month of May, 1777, he enlisted in Moore's Company, Tenth Regiment, from North Carolina, and that in June he was promoted to the rank of corporal.

According to the fireside tales told by Colonel Koen to the household in the old Koen homestead, this young soldier, then only twenty years old, was with Gates' army, that, under the valiant leadership of Morgan and Arnold, won for the newly born nation the great victory of Saratoga; and the winter of that same year — '77 — we find him sharing with Washington's army the trials and privations of the days of suffering at Valley Forge.

"I have seen the tears trickling down my grandfather's face when he told of the sufferings of that awful winter," said his granddaughter, Mrs. Temple to the writer, "and I used to wonder at seeing a grown man cry, and often I said in my childish way that war should never bring a tear in my eyes. Little did I know then that the bitterest tears I should ever shed would be caused by war, and for eighteen months during the terrible struggle between the North and the South I should mourn as dead my soldier husband, whom God in

His mercy restored to me after all hope of seeing him alive again was over."

Although the Colonial Records state that Koen enlisted for only three years in May, 1777, he must have re-enlisted in 1780, for he has left with his family a graphic description of General Lincoln's surrender of Charleston in that year, and of the horrible treatment to which the Continental troops were subjected, who found themselves prisoners of the victorious British army.

The hot climate, the wretched condition of the prison ships, the unwholesome and insufficient food, made these days of imprisonment at Charleston equal in horror to the worst days at Valley Forge. Of the 1,800 prisoners who were taken captive on May 12, 1780, only 700 survived when they were paroled, and of these our hero was one.

In what other battles or experiences Colonel Koen shared we have no record, historical or traditional, but according to his granddaughter's account, learned from his own lips, he served his country until the victory of Yorktown was won and peace was declared. And it is easy to believe that this gallant soldier who was one of the first to volunteer at Great Bridge, and who fought so bravely in many of the sharpest struggles of the great conflict, would not have been willing to lay down his arms until his country was freed from the power that had so long held it in thrall.

So we can imagine him following Greene in his retreat across the State, taking part in the battle of Guilford Courthouse, and possibly present when the proud Cornwallis was forced to surrender at Yorktown.

When the struggle at last had ended, John Koen returned to his home. During the years of his absence his plantation was managed by William Temple, whose pretty young daughter, Susannah, soon won the heart of the brave soldier, and consented to become his bride. After some years of happy married life, the young wife died, and a few years later we find John Koen making a second marriage, his bride being Christian Hollowell, of Perquimans County.

Owing to his gallant conduct in the Revolutionary War, John Koen, a few years after the war was over, was appointed Colonel of the militia in Pasquotank County, and the government awarded him a pension, which was paid until his death in 1840.

CHAPTER XII

GENERAL ISAAC GREGORY, A REVOLUTIONARY OFFICER OF PASQUOTANK-CAMDEN

During the War of the Revolution, the Albemarle Region, though threatened with invasion time and again by the British, seldom heard the tread of the enemy's army, or felt the shock of battle. For this immunity from the destruction of life and property, such as the citizens whose homes lay in the path of Cornwallis and Tarleton suffered, this section of North Carolina is largely indebted to General Isaac Gregory, one of the bravest officers who ever drew sword in defense of his native home and country.

Both Pasquotank and Camden claim this gallant officer for their son, and both have a right to that claim; for the two counties were one until 1777. In that year a petition was presented to the General Assembly by Joseph Jones, of Pasquotank, from citizens living in what is now Camden County, that the portion of Pasquotank lying on the northeast bank of the river should be formed into a separate county, and have a court-house of its own, in order to do away with the inconvenience the people of that section suffered in having to cross the river to attend court, military drills and other public gatherings. The General Assembly passed an act providing for the erection of a new county, and this county was named for Charles Pratt, Earl of Camden, a member of Parliament and Chancellor, who in the stormy days of 1765 worked for the repeal of the hated Stamp Act, and justice to the Colonies.

Before the long and bloody days of the Revolution proved his worth as a soldier, Isaac Gregory had won a prominent place in the public affairs of his county. His name first occurs in the Colonial Records in 1773, when he was elected sheriff of Pasquotank. In the same year he was appointed one of the trustees of St. Martin's Chapel in Indian Town, Currituck County, a settlement whose citizens were many of them to become honored in the civil and military history of our State.

Ever since the passing of the Stamp Act in 1765, low mutterings of the storm that was soon to sweep over the country some ten years later had disturbed the peace of the Thirteen Colonies; and events in North Carolina showed that this colony was standing shoulder to shoulder with her American sisters in their endeavor to obtain justice from England.

In 1774, John Harvey's trumpet call to the people of North Carolina to circumvent Governor Martin's attempt to deprive them of representation in the Continental Congress at Philadelphia, had resulted in the convention at New Bern, the first meeting in America at which the representatives of a colony as a whole had ever gathered in direct defiance of orders from a Royal Governor.

The next year, in April, Harvey again called a convention of the people to meet in New Bern. Again Governor Martin was defied; again, the North Carolinians, taking matters into their own hands, elected delegates to Philadelphia, and before adjourning, added Carolina's name to the association of Colonies.

Pasquotank was represented in this convention by Edward Jones, Joseph Redding, Edward Everigen, John Hearing, and Isaac Gregory. The last named, being by now an acknowledged leader in his county, was appointed by this body a member of the Committee of Safety in the Edenton District.

The path toward separation from the mother country was now being rapidly trod by the American colonies, though few, as yet, realized whither their steps were tending. In the vanguard of this march toward liberty and independence, North Carolina kept a conspicuous place. The Edenton Tea Party in October, 1774, had proved the mettle of her women. The farmers of Mecklenburg had struck the first chord in the song of independence, hardly a note of which had been sounded by the other colonies. Governor Martin had fled from New Bern, and in August, 1775, the Hillsboro Convention had organized a temporary form of government, and had placed at the head of public affairs Cornelius Harnett, who, as President of the Provincial Council, had more power in the State than is generally delegated to a governor.

In December, 1775, Lord Dunmore's attempted invasion of the State had been thwarted, largely by the aid of the Minute Men from Albemarle. Then came the famous Snow Campaign, in which the militia of the western counties joined the patriots of South Carolina in defeating the Tories of that State. And in February, 1776, the important victory at Moore's Creek Bridge had completely for a time broken the power of the Loyalists in North Carolina. There was no longer any hope of obtaining justice from England, nor, after such open and steady rebellion against the king's officers, civil and military, could there be any hope of conciliation with the mother country, save on terms too humiliating to even contemplate.

North Carolina, recognizing these facts, called another convention to meet at Halifax in April, 1776, and there sounded her defiance as a State to King and Parliament, and boldly authorized her delegates to the next Continental Congress at Philadelphia to vote for independence.

The convention then proceeded to make further preparations for the war which all now felt was inevitable. Pasquotank, in response to the call immediately issued for more troops, raised two regiments of militia. Isaac Gregory, who had been appointed Lieutenant-Colonel of the Pasquotank Militia by the Convention of 1775, was promoted and made Colonel of the Second Regiment of Pasquotank Militia, the other officers being Dempsey Burgess, Lieutenant-Colonel, Joshua Campbell, Major, and Peter Daugé, Second Major.

Independence having been declared by the Continental Congress of 1776, the thirteen Colonies, now independent States, proceeded to organize a permanent government within their several borders.

In North Carolina a State convention was called to meet at Halifax in November, 1776, to frame a constitution for the government of that State. To this convention Isaac Gregory, Henry Abbott, Devotion Davis, Dempsey Burgess and Lemuel Burgess were elected to represent Pasquotank, and Abbott was appointed on the committee to frame the constitution. By the 18th of December the work was completed and the constitution adopted, which, with amendments, is still the organic law of the State.

After Clinton's unsuccessful attempt to invade North Carolina in May, 1776, no further effort to place the State under British control was made until 1780. But during the intervening years the Carolina troops had not been idle. Their valor had been proved at Brandywine, Germantown and Stony Point, and during the winter at Valley Forge 1,450 of her soldiers shared with their comrades from the other States the hunger, cold and suffering that was the portion of Washington's army throughout those dreary months. The North Carolina troops had aided in the brave but unsuccessful attempt to drive the British from Savannah, and 5,000 of her soldiers had been sent to prevent the capture of Charleston; but the patriot forces had been unable to repulse the invaders. Savannah fell, then Charleston, and by the last of May, 1780, both Georgia and South Carolina were in the hands of the enemy, and Cornwallis was threatening North Carolina.

So great was the blow to the American cause from the loss of these Southern States, and so great the danger confronting North Carolina, that Congress ordered DeKalb, of the Continental line with the regulars from Maryland and Delaware to march to the rescue of the patriots in the South. General Gates, the reputed victor at Saratoga, was also ordered South, and put in command of the Southern forces.

For awhile the enemy remained quiet, Cornwallis delaying the devastation of South Carolina until the maturing crops should be safe. This respite gave the Carolinians time to collect their forces on the South Carolina border, in order to drive back the enemy.

Isaac Gregory, who in May, 1779, had been promoted to the office of Brigadier-General of the Edenton District, on the resignation of John Pugh Williams, was ordered to join General Caswell in South Carolina. As soon as he could collect his men, Gregory marched towards the Piedmont section, on his way to Caswell's army; and by June he was with Rutherford's Brigade at Yadkin's Ford in Rowan. Near this place the Tories had collected, some 800 strong; and Rutherford hoped, with Gregory's aid, to crush them. But to his disappointment, no opportunity was given, for General Bryan, the Tory leader, hearing of the defeat of the Loyalists at Ramseur's Mill a few days before, crossed the Yadkin and united with General MacArthur, whom Cornwallis had sent to Anson County.

By July 31 Gregory's men, with Rutherford and his brigade, were with General Caswell at The Cheraws, just across the South Carolina border. For several weeks there was much suffering among the men on account of the lack of food, for though corn was plentiful, the rivers were so high that the mills could not grind the meal.

Lord Rawdon's army was stationed near Camden, South Carolina, and Gates, who had joined Caswell on August 17, having learned that the British general was daily expecting a supply of food and stores for his men, determined to intercept the convoy and capture the supplies for his own army. In the meantime Cornwallis, unknown to Gates, had joined Lord Rawdon. Gates, ignorant of this reinforcement of Cornwallis' troops, marched leisurely towards Camden to capture the coveted stores.

The result of the battle that followed is known only too well. The American militia, panic-stricken at the furious onslaught of the enemy, threw down their arms and fled. General Gates, after a vain attempt to rally his troops, lost courage, and abandoning his forces and his stores, brought everlasting disgrace upon his name by fleeing in hot haste from the field.

But the cowardly conduct of Gates and several of the other officers of the American army, as well as many of the militia, in this disastrous battle, was offset by the heroism and courage of others; and among those who won undying fame on that fatal field, none is more worthy of praise than General Gregory.

Roger Lamb, a British officer, writing an account of the battle, and speaking of the disgraceful conduct of those officers and men whose flight from the field brought shame upon the American army, gives this account of Isaac Gregory's heroic struggle to withstand the enemy at this bloody field: "In justice to North Carolina, it should be remarked that General Gregory's brigade acquitted themselves well. They formed on the left of the Continentals, and kept the field while they had a cartridge left. Gregory himself was twice wounded by bayonets in bringing off his men, and many in his brigade had only bayonet wounds."

As to fight hand to hand with bayonets requires far more courage than to stand at a distance and fire a musket, this account of Gregory and his troops proves the bravery with which they fought during those terrible hours. General Gregory's horse was shot from under him while the battle was raging; and seeing him fall, so sure was the enemy of his death that Cornwallis in his official report of the battle, gave in his name in the list of the American officers killed on the field.

Two days after the battle of Camden, the patriots, Shelby, Clarke and Williams, defeated a band of Tories at Musgrove's Mill in South Carolina; but hearing of the disaster at Camden, these officers now withdrew from the State. Sumter's corps, near Rocky Mount, had been put to flight by Tarleton, Gates had fled the State, and only Davie's men were left between the army of Cornwallis and Charlotte, North Carolina.

Had the British General pressed on into the State, North Carolina must have inevitably fallen into the hands of the enemy. But Cornwallis delayed the invasion for nearly a month, thus giving the Carolinians time to collect their forces to repel his attempt.

The General Assembly which met in September, 1780, acting upon Governor Nash's advice, created a Board of War to assist him in conducting the military affairs of the State. This board now proceeded to put General Smallwood, of Maryland, in command of all the forces in the State, giving him authority over all the officers in the Southern army, the honor being conferred upon him on account of his gallant conduct at Camden. General Gregory was consequently ordered to hold himself in readiness to obey General Smallwood's orders, with the other officers in North Carolina.

The Board of War then proceeded to raise money, arms and men for the army that would soon be called upon to drive Cornwallis from the State. Gregory's brigade received $25,000 of the funds raised, and 150 flints and 15 guns were distributed among his soldiers.

The British now confidently expected that Cornwallis would quickly subdue North Carolina, then sweep over the State into Virginia. In order to prevent the Americans from hurrying into that State to join forces against Cornwallis, General Leslie was ordered from New York to the Chesapeake, and in October his army was stationed near South Quays in Virginia, not far from Norfolk.

The presence of Leslie's army so close to the Carolina border caused much alarm for the safety of the Albemarle section, which for the second time was in danger of invasion. General Gregory, who after the battle of Camden had joined Exum and Jarvis in front of Cornwallis, had recently returned to Albemarle. He was now ordered to take the field against Leslie, and to prevent him from entering the State. From his camp at Great Swamp, near North River, he wrote to Governor Nash in November, 1780, reporting the repulse of the enemy. He also warned the Governor that the British were planning to attack Edenton; and he set forth in his letter the blow that the capture of this town would be to the commerce of the State.

General Gregory's post at Great Swamp was no sinecure. He had only about 100 men to withstand Leslie, whose forces at Portsmouth amounted to nearly 1,000 men. His troops were poorly equipped, half naked, and ill-fed; and his situation seemed almost desperate. To add to his troubles, an attempt was made at this time by Colonel Blount, of the Edenton District, to deprive him of his command. But a Council of State, held at Camp Norfleet Mills to inquire into the matter, declared that as Colonel Blount had resigned of his own free will and accord—in favor of Gregory—he should not now take the command from him.

In spite of the troubles and perplexities that beset Gregory in the fall of 1780, he bravely held his ground; and by the end of November he wrote Governor Nash from his camp at North West that the British had abandoned Portsmouth, and had departed for parts unknown.

While these events were taking place in the East, Cornwallis, whose left wing under Ferguson had suffered a crushing defeat at King's Mountain, disappointed at the humbling of the Tories at that battle, had left North Carolina on October 12th, and returned to South Carolina. The heavy rains encountered by his army on his retreat caused much sickness among his men; and himself falling ill, he was obliged to give up his command temporarily to Lord Rawdon.

General Leslie's destination soon became known. On November 23 he had abandoned the vicinity of Norfolk, and had sailed to Wilmington, N.C., hoping to rouse the Tories in that section; but Lord Rawdon's army being now in great danger, Leslie was ordered to his assistance, and he accordingly set out for the British army near Camden. But Southern Virginia and the Albemarle region were not long to be free from the fear of invasion, for soon another British army under the command of the traitor, Benedict Arnold, sailed into Chesapeake Bay, and Gregory was again sent to keep the enemy in check.

During this campaign a serious charge was brought against Gregory, which, though soon proved to be wholly unfounded, caused the gallant officer life-long mortification and distress. The circumstances of this unfortunate occurrence were as follows:

Captain Stevens, a British officer in Arnold's corps, while sitting idly by his fire one night, "just for a joke," as he afterwards explained, wrote two notes to General Gregory, which he intended to destroy, as they were simply the product of his own imagination, and were never intended to go out of his hands.

In some unknown way these papers came into the hands of an American officer, who, deeming from their contents that Gregory was a traitor, carried them to headquarters. Their purport being made public, even Gregory's most loyal friends began to look upon him with suspicion and distrust.

The first of these two notes was as follows:

"General Gregory:

"Your well-formed plans of delivering into the hands of the British these people now in your command, gives me much pleasure. Your next, I hope, will mention place of ambuscade, and manner you wish to fall into my hands."

The second note was equally incriminating:

"General Gregory:

"A Mr. Ventriss was last night made prisoner by three or four of your people. I only wish to inform you that Ventriss could not help doing what he did in helping to destroy the logs. I myself delivered him the order from Colonel Simcox."

Great was the excitement and consternation in Gregory's brigade, and indeed throughout the American army when these notes were read. Arnold's treason early in 1780 was still fresh in the minds of all; and it was natural that the accusation now brought against General Gregory should find ready and widespread credence. Gregory was arrested and court-martialed by his own men; but his innocence was soon established, for as soon as Colonel Stevens heard of the disgrace he had unintentionally brought upon an innocent man, he hastened to make amends for his thoughtless act by a full explanation of his part in the affair. Colonel Parker, a British officer and a friend of Stevens, had been informed of the writing of the notes, and he now joined Stevens in furnishing testimony at the trial that fully exonerated the brave general from the hateful charge. But though friends and brother officers now crowded around him with sincere and cordial congratulations upon the happy termination of the affair, and with heartfelt expressions of regret at the unfortunate occurrence, the brave and gallant officer, crushed and almost heartbroken at the readiness with which his men and many of his fellow officers had accepted what seemed proofs of his guilt, never recovered from the hurt caused by the cruel charge. For though he nobly put aside his just resentment, and remained at his post of duty, guarding the Albemarle counties from danger of invasion until the withdrawal of the British troops from southeastern Virginia removed the danger, his life was ever afterwards shadowed by the mortification he had been called upon to undergo.

In February, 1781, the enemy's army in Virginia became such a source of terror to the people of that section that General Allen Jones was ordered to reinforce Gregory with troops from the Halifax District. But later that same month a greater danger confronted the patriot army in the South, and this order was countermanded. Most of the forces in the States were now hurried to the aid of General Greene, who had superseded Gates after the battle of Camden, and was leading Cornwallis an eventful chase across the Piedmont section of North Carolina. Cornwallis, after having been reinforced by General Leslie, had planned to invade North Carolina, conquer that State, march through Virginia and join Clinton in a fierce onslaught against Washington's army in the North. To foil the plans of the British officers Greene was concentrating the patriot troops in the South in the Catawba Valley, and Gregory was left with only a handful of men to hold the enemy at Norfolk in check.

In June, General Gregory's situation was so desperate that the Assembly again ordered General Allan Jones to send 400 men from Halifax District to North West Bridge to reinforce Gregory; and the latter officer was authorized to draft as many men as possible from the Edenton District.

General Jones informed the Assembly that he would send the troops as soon as possible, but that Gregory would have to provide arms, as he had no means of furnishing equipments for them.

Several engagements took place in June between the British and Americans in the Dismal Swamp region, and in one of them Gregory was repulsed and driven from his position. But in July he wrote to Colonel Blount reporting that his losses were trifling, and that he had regained his old post from the enemy. In August, 1781, a letter from General Gregory conveyed the joyful tidings that the enemy had evacuated Portsmouth. As his troops were no longer needed to guard against the danger of invasion from that direction, and as smallpox had broken out in his camp, General Gregory now released his men from duty, and they returned to their homes.

The British army that had just left Portsmouth, was now on its way to Yorktown, whither Cornwallis, after his fruitless chase of Greene, his disastrous victory at Guilford Courthouse, and his retreat to Wilmington, was now directing his army. There on the 19th of October the famous Battle of Yorktown was fought and Cornwallis and his entire army forced to surrender.

This battle virtually ended the war; but peace did not come to Carolina immediately upon the surrender. The Tories in the State kept up a constant warfare upon their Whig neighbors, and in March, 1782, General Greene, who not long after the battle of Guilford Courthouse had won a decisive victory at Eutaw Springs, and was still in South Carolina, sent the alarming intelligence to the towns on the coast that the British had sent four vessels from Charleston harbor to plunder and burn New Bern and Edenton. To meet this unexpected emergency, General Rutherford was ordered to quell the Tories in the Cape Fear section, who were terrorizing the people in that region. And in April, 1782, General Gregory received orders from General Burke to take 500 men to Edenton for the defense of that town, and to notify Count de Rochambeau as soon as the enemy should appear in Albemarle Sound. In August no sign of the British ships had as yet been seen, though the coast towns were still in daily dread of their arrival. Governor Martin, who had succeeded Burke, wrote Gregory to purchase whatever number of vessels the Edenton merchants considered necessary for the protection of the town, to buy cannon and to draft men to man the boats.

But Edenton was spared the horror of a second raid such as she had suffered in 1781. In December, 1782, the British army in South Carolina, which since the battle of Eutaw Springs had been hemmed in at Charleston by General Greene, finally embarked for England. The ships that had been keeping the towns near the coast in North Carolina in terror, departed with them, and the States that had for so many long and bitter years been engaged in the terrific struggle with England, were left to enjoy the fruits of their splendid victory without further molestation from the enemy.

In September, 1783, the Treaty of Peace was signed by Great Britain, and the United States, separately and individually, were declared to be "free, sovereign and independent States."

General Gregory's services to his State did not end with the war. Eight times from 1778 to 1789, we find him representing Camden County in the State Senate, serving on important committees, and lending the weight of his influence to every movement tending toward the prosperity and welfare of the State. In the local affairs of his neighborhood he also took a prominent part. In 1789 the Currituck Seminary was established at Indian Town, and Isaac Gregory and his friend and brother officer, Colonel Peter Daugé, were appointed on the board of trustees of this school, which for many years was one of the leading educational institutions of the Albemarle section.

General Gregory lived at the Ferebee place in Camden County in a large brick house, known then, as now, as Fairfax Hall. The old building is still standing, a well known landmark in the county.

A letter from James Iredell to his wife, written while this famous North Carolina judge was a guest at Fairfax, gives a pleasant account of an evening spent in General Gregory's home with Parson Pettigrew and Gideon Lamb, and also of the kindness and hospitality of the Camden people.

In volume 2 of the Iredell letters this description of General Gregory's personal appearance is given:

"A lady, who remembers General Gregory well, says that he was a large, fine looking man. He was exceedingly polite, had a very grand air, and in dress was something of a fop." In the same volume the following interesting account of an incident in the life of the famous General is found: "General Gregory lived in his latter years so secluded a life and knew so little of events beyond his own family circle, that he addressed to a lady, the widow of Governor Stone, a letter making a formal proposal of marriage, full six months after her death."

General Isaac Gregory was the son of General William Gregory, an officer who took a prominent part in the French and Indian Wars. He married Miss Elizabeth Whedbee, and had two children, Sarah and Matilda. Sarah married Dempsey Burgess, of Camden, and Matilda married a young German, John Christopher Ehringhaus. Many of the descendants of this brave Revolutionary officer are living in the Albemarle region to-day, and claim with pride this ancestor, who, as Captain Ashe in his History of North Carolina says, "was one of the few who won honor at Camden, and whose good fame was never tarnished by a single unworthy action."

FAIRFAX, CAMDEN COUNTY, THE HOME OF GENERAL GREGORY

The Sir Walter Raleigh Chapter of the Daughters of the Revolution have within the past year obtained from the United States government a simple stone which they have had placed to mark the grave of this gallant officer, who lies buried in the family graveyard at Fairfax.

CHAPTER XIII

PERQUIMANS COUNTY—"LAND OF BEAUTIFUL WOMEN," AND THE COLONIAL TOWN OF HERTFORD

From its hidden source in the southern fringe of the far-famed Dismal Swamp, the Perquimans River, lovely as its Indian name, which, being interpreted, signifies "the land of beautiful women," comes winding down. Past marshes green with flags and rushes and starred with flowers of every hue, through forests dense with pine and cypress, with gum and juniper, the amber waters of the ancient stream pursue their tranquil way. Lazily, but steadily and untiringly, the river journeys on in obedience to the eternal, insistent call of the sea, till its waves, meeting and mingling with those of the great sound and its numerous tributaries, finally find their way through the sand bars that bound our coast, to the stormy Atlantic.

Save for the fields of corn and cotton that lie along its banks, and an occasional sawmill whose whirring wheels break at long intervals the silence of its wooded shores, the peaceful river through the greater part of its way is undisturbed by signs of man's presence. Only twice in its course do its banks resound to the hum of town and village life, once when shortly emerging from the Great Swamp, the river in its winding flows by the sleepy little Quaker village of Belvidere; and again when its tranquility is suddenly broken by the stir and bustle of mill and factory, upon whose existence depends the prosperity of the old colonial town of Hertford. There, the river, suddenly as wide awake as the beautiful town by which it flows, changes its narrow, tortuous, leisurely course, and broadening out from a slender stream, sweeps on to the sea, a river grown, whose shores from this point on lie apart from each other a distance of more than a mile.

Of all the streams that flow down to the sea from Albemarle, none exceeds in beauty or historic interest the lovely Perquimans River. On its eastern banks lies Durant's Neck, the home of George Durant, the first settler in our State, who in 1661 left his Virginia home and came into Albemarle; and being well pleased with the beauty and fertility of fair Wikacome, was content to abide thenceforth in that favored spot.

On the banks of the streams flowing on either side of Wikacome, roamed an Indian tribe, the Yeopims, whose great chief Kilcokonen gave to George Durant the first deed for land ever recorded in our State. Durant, his friend and comrade, Samuel Pricklove, and their families and servants, proved to be the vanguard of a long procession of settlers, who, following the footsteps of these first pioneers, made their homes upon the shores of the Albemarle streams. Soon the dense forests that stretched down to the river brinks fell beneath the axe of these home-seekers, and small farms and great plantations fringed the borders of the streams.

At the narrows of the Perquimans, where the waters widen into a broad, majestic river, a sturdy pioneer, Henry Phillips (or Phelps) had built his home. Thither in the spring of 1672, came a missionary, William Edmundson, a friend and follower of George Fox, who some years before had over in England founded the Society of Friends. Henry Phelps was a member of this Society also, and the meeting between the two godly men was a joyful one.

During the ten years that had passed since the Indian Chief had signed his first grant of land to the white man, the settlers of Albemarle had had no opportunity of assembling together for public worship. Phelps, knowing how gladly the call would be answered, at the bidding of Edmundson, summoned such of his friends and neighbors as he could reach, to his home, to hear the Word preached by this zealous man of God.

Not since the days of little Virginia Dare had a body of Christian men and women met together in Carolina to offer in public worship their prayer and praises to the loving Father, who had led them safely over storm-tossed waters, through tangled wilderness, into this Land of Promise. Rough and uncultured as most of the congregation were, they listened quietly and reverently to the good missionary, and received the Word with gladness. There were present at the meeting "one Tems and his wife," who earnestly entreated Edmundson to hold another service at their home three miles away. So the next day he journeyed to the home of Tems, and there another "blessed meeting" was held; and there was founded a Society whose members were to be for many years the most prominent religious body in the State.

In the fall of 1672, the hearts of the members of this infant church were gladdened by the tidings that George Fox himself was on his way to visit the little band of brethren in the wilds of Carolina. One cool, crisp October morning, the great preacher arrived. Again was the home of Phelps chosen for the meeting; but so great was the crowd that gathered to hear him that the house would not hold the congregation. Standing a little distance from Phelps' simple dwelling were two great cypress trees. Close down by the water's edge they grew, their feathery branches shading the rippling waves, and shielding the listeners from the glare of a sun whose rays had not yet lost their summer's heat. Under one of these trees the preacher stood, and spoke to the assembled crowd as the Spirit gave him utterance. It was a "tender meeting," as Fox reports in his letters describing his stay in Perquimans. Many who were present became converts to the faith of Fox and Edmundson; and Perquimans County and her sister, Pasquotank, became for many years the stronghold of the Society of Friends in Carolina.

For a number of years after George Fox's visit to Perquimans, the Quakers were the only religious body in the colony that regularly assembled its members together for divine service. Their ministers were for the most part from the congregation itself; no salary was demanded by them; and the home of some Friends was the scene of their religious meetings. In a new country where ready money is a scarce commodity, a church that could be conducted without any expenditure of cash could more easily take root, than one whose existence depended upon a certain amount, however small, of filthy lucre.

The Lords Proprietors, members for the most part of the Church of England, were too intent upon extracting wealth from their colony in Carolina to be willing to expend any of their gains for the good of the colonists. Disregarding the petitions of their officers in Albemarle, who saw the great need for missionaries in the struggling settlements, they refused to become responsible for the salary of a minister.

But after a while the Society for the Propagation of the Gospel in foreign parts took hold of the matter, and in 1702 a church was built in Chowan, near where Edenton now stands. By 1709 Rev. Mr. Gordon, who was one of the two ministers sent out by the S.P.G., writes to the secretary of the Society from Perquimans:

"In Perquimans there is a compact little church, built with care and express, and better than that in Chowan. It continues yet unfinished, by reason of the death of Major Swann, 1707, who fostered the building of this church."

Among the vestrymen of this new parish may be found the following names: Francis Forbes, Colonel Maurice Moore, Captain Hecklefield, Thomas Hardy, Captain Richard Saunderson, Henry Clayton, Joseph Jessups, Samuel Phelps and Richard Whedbee. Most of these gentlemen were men of note in the colony, and many of their descendants are now living in Perquimans County.

That the wealthy planters in Albemarle felt a certain responsibility for the spiritual welfare of their slaves, was shown by the fact that master and slave alike gathered together to join in the services held by the early missionaries of the Church of England; and that the master willingly allowed his servant to share in the blessings of the sacraments of the church. A letter from Rev. Mr. Taylor, written from Perquimans in 1719, records that he had just "baptized a young woman, slave of Mr. Duckinfield, to whom I have taught the whole of the church catechism."

But the letter further reveals that our early colonists cherished their worldly possessions fully as fondly as their descendants, who pursue with avidity the chase after the dollar. And when it came to the question of the slave's spiritual welfare, or the master's temporal prosperity, the master did not hesitate to show which he considered of the most importance. For, as Mr. Taylor writes, when it was rumored in 1719 that the General Assembly of that year had decreed that all baptized slaves should be set free; and when, immediately, and by a strange coincidence, the reverend gentleman was suddenly besieged by bands of men and women, all loudly clamoring to receive the rite of holy baptism, Duckinfield and others of the planters prudently restrained the poor darkies from entering the church's folds until that law could be repealed.

In secular as well as religious affairs, Perquimans precinct in those early days took an active part. Men of political and social prominence resided within her borders, and at their homes, for lack of other shelter for public gatherings, much of the business of the colony, legislative and judicial, was transacted.

As early as 1677 the population of Albemarle had grown so numerous that the settlers found themselves strong enough to successfully resist the oppressive rule of the unworthy governors set over them by the Lords Proprietors. And in that year, led by John Culpeper and George Durant, a revolt against the tyrannical Miller, which began in Pasquotank, spread through the surrounding precincts.

Among the men from Perquimans who took part in this disturbance, known in history as Culpeper's Rebellion, were George Durant, Alexander Lillington, Samuel Pricklove, Jenkins, Sherrell and Greene. So successfully did they and their comrades strive against Miller's tyranny, that that worthy was driven out of Carolina, and the reins of government fell into the hands of Culpeper and Durant. And at the home of the latter on Durant's Neck, a fair and equitable people's government was organized, the first of the kind framed in America.

Alexander Lillington, who lent the weight of his wealth and influence to the people in their struggle against Miller, was a rich planter who in 1698 bought a tract of land from Stephen Pane and John Foster, on Yeopim Creek, and soon became one of the leading men in the colony. His descendants moved to New Hanover, and a namesake of his in later years won for himself undying fame at the Battle of Moore's Creek Bridge.

At the homes of Captain John Hecklefield and Captain Richard Saunderson, the General Assembly and the Governor's Council often convened. The famous Glover-Cary controversy was temporarily settled at the home of the former, by the Assembly of 1708, while Captain Saunderson's dwelling sheltered the Assembly of 1715, whose important acts were for the first time formally recorded and published. The courts were frequently held at the home of Dinah Maclenden, and James Thickpenny. James Oates, Captain James

Cole and Captain Anthony Dawson also bore their share in entertaining the judicial assemblies.

As the population of the colony increased, facilities for carrying on commerce and for traveling through the country became one of the crying needs of the day. The numerous rivers of Albemarle made provision for ferries imperative, and as early as 1700, we find record made of "Ye ferre over ye mane road" in Perquimans. In 1706 it is recorded that Samuel Phelps was appointed "Keeper of ye Toll Boke at ye Head of Perquimans River."

A council held at the home of Captain Saunderson in 1715 ordered: "That for the better convenience of people passing through the country, a good and sufficient ferry be duly kept and attended over Perquimans River, from Mrs. Anne Wilson's to James Thickpenny, and that Mrs. Wilson do keep the same, and that no other persons presume to ferry over horse or man within five miles above or below that place."

As time went on, the crowds attending the courts and Assemblies became too large to be accommodated in private dwellings. As early as 1722, the General Assembly ordered a court-house to be built at Phelps Point, now the town of Hertford, and tradition states that the old building was erected on the point near the bridge, where the home of Mr. Thomas McMullan now stands.

One of the most interesting spots in Perquimans County is the strip of land lying between the Perquimans and the Yeopim rivers, known as Harvey's Neck. This was the home of the Harveys, men who for over a century bore an important part in the history of our State. It was in older days, as now, a fair and fertile land. Herds of deer wandered through its forests; and great flocks of swan and wild geese floated upon its silver streams, feeding upon the sweet grass which then grew in those rivers. The waters were then salt, but with the choking up of the inlets that let in the saline waves of the Atlantic, the grass disappeared, and with it the wild fowl who wintered there.

Of all the members of the famous Harvey family whose homes were builded on this spot, none proved more worthy of the fame he won than John Harvey, son of Thomas Harvey and Elizabeth Coles.

Elected when just of age to the Assembly of 1746, he continued to serve his State in a public capacity until his death in 1775.

Resisting the tyrannical endeavor of Governor Dobbs to tax the people against their rights, he nevertheless stood by the same governor in his efforts to raise men and money for the French and Indian War. Serving as Speaker of the House in 1766, he took an active part in opposing the Stamp Act, and boldly declared in the Assembly that North Carolina would not pay those taxes. In the Assembly of 1769 he proposed that Carolina should form a Non-Importation Association; and when Governor Tryon thereupon angrily dismissed the Assembly and ordered its members home, Harvey called a convention independent of the Governor, and the association was formed.

When Governor Martin refused to call the Assembly of 1774, for fear that it would elect delegates to the Continental Congress, John Harvey declared: "Then the people will call an Assembly themselves"; and following their intrepid leader, the people did call the convention of 1774, elected their delegates to Philadelphia, and openly and boldly joined and led their sister colonies in the gigantic struggle with the mother country that now began.

In the time of Boston's need, when her ports were closed by England's orders, and her people were threatened with starvation, John Harvey and Joseph Hewes together caused the ship "Penelope" to be loaded with corn and meal, flour and pork, which they solicited from the generous people of Albemarle, and sent it with words of cheer and sympathy to their brethren in the New England town. In 1775 Harvey again braved the anger of the Royal Governor and called another people's convention, whose purpose and work was to watch and circumvent the tyrant in his endeavor to crush the patriots in the State.

"The Father of the Revolution" in Carolina, he was to his native State what Patrick Henry was to Virginia, in the early days of the Revolution, and what Hancock and Adams were to Massachusetts. His untimely death, in 1775, caused by a fall from a horse, was deeply mourned by patriots throughout the land.

Among other eminent sons of Perquimans during the Revolutionary period the names of Miles Harvey, Colonel of the regiment from that county; William Skinner, Lieutenant-Colonel of the same regiment; Thomas Harvey, Major, and Major Richard Clayton, are recorded in history. Among the delegates to the People's Convention called by Harvey and Johnston we find the Harveys, Whedbees, Blounts, Skinners and Moores, men whose names were prominent then as now in the social and political life of the State.

As time went on, Phelps Point at the Narrows of the Perquimans River became so thickly populated that by June, 1746, a petition was presented to the General Assembly, praying for an act to be passed to lay out 100 acres of land in Perquimans, including Phelps Point, for a town and a town commons.

But a disturbance arose in the State about that time concerning the right of the northern counties to send five delegates each to the Assembly, while the southern counties were allowed to send only two. Governor Gabriel Johnson sided with the southern section, and ordered the Assembly to meet at Wilmington in November, 1746, on which occasion he and the southern delegates proposed to make a strong fight to reduce the representation from the Albemarle counties.

The northern counties, tenaciously clinging to their rights, established in the early days of the colony when the counties south of Albemarle Sound had not been organized, refused to send delegates to this Assembly; whereupon that body, though a majority of its members were absent, passed an act reducing the representation from the Albemarle region to two members from each county. Indignant at this act, which they considered illegal, the citizens in the northern counties refused to subscribe to it, and for eight years declined to send any delegates at all to the Assembly; and the bill for establishing a town in Perquimans was heard from no more until the trouble between the two sections was settled.

Finally the people of Albemarle sent a petition to George III, praying him to restore their rights in the General Assembly, and the King graciously granted their request. In 1758 an Assembly met at New Bern, at which delegates from all sections of the colony were present; and in answer to a petition presented by John Harvey, it passed an act for the erection of a town at Phelps Point in Perquimans County.

The little village was called Hertford, a word of Saxon origin, signifying Red Ford. It was named for the Marquis of Hertford, an English noble who moved for the repeal of the Stamp Act in 1766, and who was ambassador at Paris in the reign of George III, and Lord Lieutenant of Ireland.

The settlement at Phelps Point was already an important rendezvous for the dwellers in the county. The cypress trees under which Fox had stood and preached to the little band of brethren still stood, as they stand to-day, bending lovingly over the stream, close to the end of the point. A little Church of England chapel farther down had since 1709 been the center of the religious life of its members in the county, and the court-house on the point since 1722 had been the scene of the political and judicial gatherings in Perquimans.

The Assembly of 1762, realizing the importance of the little town to the community, decreed that a public ferry should be established "from Newby's Point to Phelp's Point where the court-house now stands," and in 1766 Seth Sumner, William Skinner, Francis Nixon, John Harvey and Henry Clayton were appointed trustees of the ferry; a three-penny tax was laid on all taxable persons to defray the expenses of the ferry, and "All persons crossing to attend vestry meetings, elections, military musters, court martials and sessions of the court" were to be carried over free of charge.

The site of the town, described in Colonial Records as "healthy, pleasantly situated, well watered and commodious for commerce," was the property of John Phelps, who gave his consent to the laying off of 100 acres for the town on condition that he should retain his own house and lot, and four lots adjoining him. The public ferry having fallen into his hands, the further condition was made that the town should allow no ferry other than his to be run so long as he complied with the ferry laws. The subscribers for the lots were ordered to build within three years, one well-framed or brick house at least 16 feet square; and in one month from purchase, were to pay the trustees the sum of 45 shillings for each lot.

As early as 1754, before the little settlement began to assume the airs of a town, the old Eagle Tavern still standing on Church street, was a registered hotel; and there when court week appeared on the calendar, the representative men of the county and the surrounding precincts would gather.

Quiet Quaker folk from Piney Woods, eight miles down from Newby's Point, Whites and Nicholsons, Albertsons, Newbys and Symmes, jogged along the country roads behind their sleek, well-fed nags, to answer with serene yea or nay the questions asked on witness stand or in jury room. Powdered and bewigged judge and lawyer, high and mighty King's officers from Edenton or New Bern, or Bath, brilliant in gay uniform, rolled ponderously thither in cumbersome coaches. Leaving their great plantations on the adjoining necks in the hands of their overseers, Harveys and Skinners, Blounts and Whedbees, Winslows and Gordons, Nixons and Woods and Leighs, dashed up to the doors of the tavern on spirited steeds. Hospitable townsfolk hurried to and fro, greeting the travelers, and causing mine host of the inn much inward concern, lest their cordial invitation lure from his door the guest whose bill he could see, in his mind's eye, pleasantly lengthen, as the crowded court docket slowly cleared.

Very sure were the guests at the tavern that horse and man would be well cared for by the genial landlord; for the law required that the host of Eagle Tavern should give ample compensation for the gold he pocketed. When business was ended, the strangers within his gates wended their way homeward. No skimping of the bill of fare, no inattention to the comfort of the wayfarer did the landlord dare allow, lest his license be taken from him for violation of the tavern laws.

Many an illustrious guest the ancient inn has known, and a story cherished by the Hertford people ascribes to the quaint old structure the honor of having on one occasion sheltered beneath its roof the illustrious "Father of his Country," George Washington.

EAGLE TAVERN, HERTFORD, NORTH CAROLINA

Whether our first President came to Hertford on business connected with lands in the Dismal Swamp in which he was interested, or whether he tarried at the old tavern while on his triumphal journey through the South in 1791, no one now knows, but the room is still shown, and the tale still told of the great man's stay therein.

Diagonally across the street from the Eagle Tavern, at the end of the yard enclosing the old Harvey home, may be seen two great stones which are said to mark the grave of a mighty Indian chief. Possibly Kilcokonen, friend of George Durant, lies buried there. The Hertford children in olden days, when tales of ghost and goblin were more readily believed than they are to-day, used to thrill with delicious fear whenever in the dusk of the evening they passed the spot, and warily they would step over the stones, half-dreading, half-hoping to see, as legend said was possible, the spirit of the old warrior rise from the grave, swinging his gory tomahawk and uttering his blood-chilling war cry.

During the long years that have passed since the white man came into Albemarle, old Perquimans has borne an enviable part in making the history of our State.

Hertford itself felt little of the fury of the storm of the War of Secession, though during the awful cataclysm the peaceful Perquimans was often disturbed by the gunboats of the Northern Army. One brief battle was fought in the town, in which one man was killed on each side. And the old residents still love to boast of the heroism shown by the courageous Hertford women, who, while the skirmish was going on, came out on their piazzas, and, heedless of the shot and shell flying thick and fast around them, cheered on the soldiers battling to defend their homes.

A ball from one of the gunboats on the river, while this skirmish was taking place, went through one of the houses down near the shore and tore the covering from the bed on which the mistress of the house had just been lying.

The cruel war at last was over, the darker days of Reconstruction passed heavily and stressfully by; the South began to recover from the ruin wrought by the awful struggle and its aftermath; and in the quiet years that followed, the Spirit of God brooded over her rivers, hills and plains, and brought peace and prosperity to the troubled land. Her farms were tilled again, the wheels of mills and factories were set whirling, and new business enterprises offered to the laboring man opportunities to earn a fair living.

And the old colonial town of Hertford, sharing with her sister towns and cities in the Southland the prosperity for which her children for many weary, painful years had so bravely and manfully striven, sees the dawn of a new day, bright with the promise of a happy future for her sons and daughters.

CHAPTER XIV

CURRITUCK, THE HAUNT OF THE WILD FOWL

Currituck County is known the country over as the sportsman's paradise. Thither when the first sharp frost gives warning that the clear autumn skies will soon be banked with gray snow clouds, the wild fowl from the far North come flocking. And as the swift-winged procession skims through the starry skies, and the hoarse cry of the aerial voyagers resounds over head, then do the dwellers in eastern Albemarle know for a surety that the year is far spent, and the winter days close at hand.

Guided by unerring instinct, the feathered tribes of the North pursue "through the boundless sky their certain flight" till the shallow waters of Currituck Sound and its reedy shores greet their eager sight. There they find the wild celery and other aquatic plants upon which they love to feed, growing in abundance; and there they make their winter home "and rest and scream among their fellows," preferring the risk of death at the hands of the sportsman to the certain starvation that would confront them in their native Arctic clime.

Vast as are to-day the clouds of wild fowl that every year descend upon the shores and waters of Currituck, their numbers were far greater in years long gone, before the white man with shot and gun came roving among the reedy marshes. Long before George Durant's advent into the State, the Indians with that aptness for nomenclature for which they are noted, had given to this haunt of the wild fowl the name of "Coretonk," or Currituck, as now called, in imitation of the cry of the feathered visitors.

But not alone as the winter home of the winged creatures of the Northern wilds was Currituck noted in the early days of our State. This county, formerly much larger than it is to-day, for many years embraced the region known as Dare County, and to Currituck belongs the distinction of having once included within its borders the spot upon which Raleigh's colonies tried to establish their homes.

The history of that event is too well known to bear repetition. The story of Amadas' and Barlowe's expedition, of Ralph Lane's bold adventures in exploration of Albemarle Sound, Chowan River and Chesapeake Bay, of the return of his disappointed colony to England in Drake's vessels, and the tragic fate of little Virginia Dare and of John White's colony, have all been told in fiction, song and verse.

The failure of Raleigh's colonies to establish a permanent settlement in the New World discouraged the English for many years from making any further attempts to settle America. From 1590, the date of Governor White's return to Roanoke, and of his unsuccessful search for the "lost colony," that lovely island for many years disappears from the white man's gaze; and save for a few scattered, unrecorded settlements in northern Albemarle, Carolina itself was almost unknown to the world.

But in September, 1654, according to the Colonial Records, a young fur trader from Virginia had the misfortune to lose his sloop in which he was about to embark for the purpose of trading with the Indians in the Albemarle country. For reasons not stated he supposed she had gone to Roanoke, so he hired a small boat, and with three companions set out in search of the runaway vessel. "They entered at Coratoke Inlet, ten miles to the north of Cape Henry," so reads the ancient chronicle, "and so went to Roanoke Island, where, or near thereabouts, they found the Great Commander of those parts with his Indians a-hunting, who received them civilly and showed them the ruins of Sir Walter Raleigh's fort, from which I received a sure token of their being there."

A few months before this journey of the young fur trader, Charles II had bestowed upon eight of his favorites all the territory in America lying between the thirty-first and thirty-sixth parallels of latitude, a princely gift indeed, and worthy of the loyal friends who had devoted their lives and fortunes to the Stuart cause during the dark days when that cause seemed hopelessly lost. This grant embraced the land adjacent to the north shore of Albemarle Sound, and extending to Florida; but it failed to include a strip of territory about thirty miles broad, lying between the thirty-sixth degree and the Virginia line. In this fertile region George Durant and other settlers had as early as 1661 established their homes, buying from Kilcokonen, the great Chief of the Yeopims, their right to the lands; and there these hardy pioneers were swiftly converting the primeval wilderness into fertile and productive fields.

Governor Berkeley, of Virginia, looked with covetous eye upon this fair strip of land, and with a view to planting settlements there in order to establish Virginia's claim to the territory, he had offered in the name of King Charles extensive grants in this region to planters who would bring a certain number of people into Albemarle. In 1663 Berkeley granted to John Harvey 600 acres of land "lying in a small creek called Curratuck (probably Indian Creek to-day), falling into the River Kecoughtancke (now North River), which falls in the Carolina River (known to-day as Albemarle Sound). The land was given Mr. Harvey for bringing into the colony twelve new settlers."

Many other settlers in this region had acquired their lands by patents from Virginia; but after the King's gift to his friends, Berkeley, himself one of the Lords Proprietors, was no longer desirous to consider the Albemarle region a part of the Virginia Colony; and henceforth the grants of land were all issued in the name of the Lords Proprietors. For several years, however, the Albemarle counties were really separate, and to all practical purposes, independent territory. The proprietors had no legal claim to the region, and there was nothing in Virginia's charter to show that she could rightfully lay claim to it. Nevertheless the proprietors did claim it, and authorized Berkeley to appoint a governor for that region. Berkeley therefore journeyed into the settlement, organized a government, and appointed Drummond Governor of Albemarle.

In 1665 the Lords, realizing the confusion that would arise unless their claim to the land was made good, induced the King to include Albemarle in their grant.

But Virginia was by no means ready to relinquish her claim to this promising settlement, and after Berkeley's day a long struggle began between the Royal Governors of that colony over the question as to who should collect the rents and taxes from the inhabitants of this disputed tract. As late as 1689 the quarrel was still going on, and the Governor and Council of Virginia appealed to William and Mary to restrain the Governor of North Carolina from collecting taxes in Currituck County; and the question of the boundary line between Virginia and Carolina still being uncertain, the sovereigns were asked to have the bounds surveyed and settled.

Not for many years was this request regarded, though in 1711 commissioners from Virginia went to Currituck to meet those from Carolina for the purpose of surveying the land and establishing the boundary between the two colonies. For some reason the Carolina commissioners failed to appear, and not till 1728 did the work of settling the disputed boundaries really begin. In March of that year commissioners from the two colonies met on the north shore of Currituck Inlet, and a cedar post on the seashore was fixed as the beginning of the line. The result of the survey was that many thousand acres and several hundred people whom Virginia had claimed were found to be in the Albemarle District.

This was naturally a great disappointment to Virginia, and equally a matter of rejoicing to Carolina, not only on account of the extra territory and inhabitants she now could lawfully claim, but because Currituck Inlet, the only entrance from the sea north of Roanoke Island, was thereafter indisputably thrown within her borders. This inlet, now closed by the shifting sands that form the long sand bars on the Carolina coast, was of great importance in the early days of the colony, forming an entrance from the sea to the sound through which the trading vessels could slip. So necessary was this inlet to the commerce of the colony that in 1726 the General Assembly ordered that the powder money accruing to the government by vessels coming into Currituck Inlet should be appropriated for beaconing and staking out the channel at that entrance. But by 1731, the steady beating of the waves on the coast had deposited a bank of sand at the inlet. Governor Burrington wrote to the Board of Trade that it was no longer possible for large vessels to enter there, nor at Roanoke Inlet, which had also become so dangerous that no one cared to use it, but that the vessels now were obliged to go around by Ocracoke Inlet to make their exit and entrance from and into Albemarle Sound. The closing of the inlet was such a serious misfortune to the State that time and again efforts were made to reopen it, and the Assembly of 1761 appropriated money for that purpose. But "man's control stops with the sea"; the waves continued to drop their burden of sand at the entrance to the inlet, and finally the attempt was abandoned. The great Atlantic had made the entrance, and the same force had closed it, seemingly, forever, though small sloops still slipped in and out over the bar until 1821, when it was entirely closed. So necessary was an outlet to the sea to the people of the Albemarle region, that the Assembly of 1786 passed an act providing for the digging of a canal from Currituck Sound to the head of North River; from thence vessels could go up North River and into Elizabeth River, and on to Norfolk, and so to the sea. This proposed plan was not carried out until many years later; for it was not until almost 1858 that the Albemarle and Chesapeake Canal, following closely the route proposed in 1786, was dug, though long before that date the Dismal Swamp Canal had been opened, and a flourishing traffic was carried on between Virginia and Carolina waters.

A traveler in eastern Carolina, writing for *Harper's Magazine* in 1858, an account of his journeyings in the Albemarle region, gives a most interesting description of his trip on the Albemarle and Chesapeake Canal. The Calypso was the first steamer to go through the canal, and on her maiden journey from Norfolk to Currituck County in 1858, she was the observed of all observers. Furthermore, continues Mr. Bruce, the writer of the article, who stopped at Currituck Courthouse for several days, "We must say that for average culture, intelligence and physical vigor, the people of this 'kingdom by the sea' will hold their own with most other communities, North or South."

Currituck being the sea frontier of Albemarle, her waterways were naturally of prime importance to the State; but other matters of as great importance are found in reading the annals of this wind-blown, wave-washed county. In religious affairs we find that she early begins to make history. In 1708 Governor Glover wrote to the Bishop of London: "Pasquotank and Currituck are now under the care of Rev. James Adams, to their general satisfaction, to whom they have presented the small provision of 30 pounds a year." In 1710 Rev. James Adams informed the S.P. G.A. that he had been living for over a year in the home of a Mr. Richard Saunderson, a former member of the Governor's Council, who had made a will in which, after his own and his wife's death, he had left considerable legacy for the encouragement of a minister in Currituck Parish, where he lived, namely: "A good plantation with all the houses and furniture, slaves, and their increase, and stock of cows, sheep and horses and hogs, with their increase forever." This was later declared void by the courts on account of Sanderson's incapacity.

So acceptable did Mr. Adams prove to the parish, that in 1710 the vestry wrote a letter of thanks to Thomas, Archbishop of Canterbury, thanking him for sending this godly clergyman of the Church of England to the parish. In 1712, on the death of Mr. Adams, the Rev. Mr. Rainsford was sent to take his place. He wrote back to England that on reaching Currituck he found a small chapel at Indian Town, and there in June of that year he "preached to vast crowds" that came to hear him.

In 1715 a legally appointed vestry was organized for the parish of Currituck, among the most prominent of whose members were Richard Saunderson, Colonel William Reed, Foster Jarvis, William Swann, and William Williams. The services of the Church of England were conducted in the county during those early days with as much regularity as the scattered congregations and the lack of facilities for traveling in that water-bound region permitted. In 1774 the General Assembly passed an act to establish St. Martin's chapel at Belleville, and Isaac Gregory, Peter Daugé and a Mr. Ferebee were appointed to take this matter in charge. In educational matters Currituck was wonderfully alert in colonial days for a county so inaccessible from the rest of the State. Probably the most noted of her schools was the Indian Town Academy built in 1761 by William Ferebee, one of the most prominent men in North Carolina, on his plantation, called by the Indians "Culong," and by the whites, "Indian Town." Many of the students at this academy were in later days to be counted among the State's most famous and useful men. William Ferebee's family alone furnished six members of the Legislature, three Revolutionary officers, and one Colonel in the Confederacy in the War of Secession. For a hundred years this famous old school kept up its career of usefulness, but in the so-called "negro raid" of 1863 it met the fate that befell so many of the South's cherished institutions during the dark days of 1861-1865, and was reduced to ashes by the incendiary's torch.

Another well known school in Indian Town, the most prominent settlement in Currituck in colonial days, was the Currituck Seminary of Learning, which was built in 1789, and which numbered among its trustees Isaac Gregory, Peter Daugé, and William Ferebee. This building served the triple purpose of school, church and Masons' Hall, the upper story being used for holding church service, and by the Masons for their meetings, and the lower for the school. The principal of this school was called the provost, a high-sounding title which must have made even the most insignificant of pedagogues feel proud and important. Among the teachers employed at this institution during the later years of its existence was Ezekiel Gilman, of Massachusetts, a graduate of Harvard, who came to Currituck in 1840 and who taught in Currituck and Camden fifty consecutive years. Mr. Gilman is still well and affectionately remembered by citizens of these counties, who as lads were fortunate enough to be his pupils. Though somewhat eccentric in manner and dress, he was a man of deep learning, whose kindness of heart was proverbial throughout the counties which were the scene of his labors.

When the storm of the Revolutionary War broke over the American Colonies, the men of Currituck came gallantly to the front, and with comrade soldiers from the other colonies doggedly and persistently fought the foe till the last British trooper was driven from the land, and independence was not only declared, but won. Few counties in the State gave more freely of her sons than did this county by the sea. Few can show a longer list of brave and gallant officers. Among the most noted of these were the three sons of William Ferebee, of Culong Plantation, Joseph, William and Samuel. Joseph was a Lieutenant in Colonel Jarvis' Tenth North Carolina Militia, and was at Valley Forge during the terrible winter of 1777-'78. There is a family tradition that he killed General Fordyce, of the British Army, at the Battle of Great Bridge, near Norfolk. William was appointed Captain in the Seventh Regiment of Continentals from North Carolina, and was later a member of the Convention of 1789, which ratified the Federal Constitution. Samuel Ferebee served as sergeant and ensign in the companies of Captain William Russell and Colonel Samuel Jarvis. He volunteered in Captain Joseph Ferebee's company, was ensign under Captain James Phillips, and was commissioned lieutenant, and collected troops by order of General Gregory for Baron Von Steuben. Samuel Ferebee was also the last surviving member of the Fayetteville Convention, which ratified the Federal Constitution. He was married three times, and as the family chronicle quaintly puts it, "was always married on Sunday and on the fourteenth day of the month."

Among the prominent families of Currituck during the colonial and Revolutionary days, as well as in our own times, was the Jarvis family, whose members have been men of note in the State since her history began.

At the two conventions, called at New Bern by John Harvey, in 1774-'75, Samuel Jarvis represented his county, and he also figured prominently in the Halifax Convention that framed our State Constitution. In 1775 he was appointed Colonel of the Minute Men from Currituck, in 1777 he was the recruiting officer from his county, and in 1779 he received his commission as Colonel of the militia, by the advice of the Governor's Council, in place of Colonel Perkins, who had recently died. During this year Jarvis wrote to Governor Ashe, asking that he would grant the petition of the men living on the "Banks," who had asked to be excused from enlisting. The dwellers on the coast were exposed to attacks from the enemy, and should the husbands and fathers of that section of the county be forced to the field, their homes would be defenceless. How great the danger was had been realized a few days before Jarvis wrote this letter, for a British ship had entered the inlet, burned two vessels belonging to the patriots, and killed the cattle in the nearby marshes. The Governor granted the petition, and seeing the peril to which the dwellers on the "Banks" were exposed, he ordered ammunition and food to be sent to Jarvis for their use and protection.

The names of Thomas Jarvis, Judge of the Admiralty Court of Currituck, and later Lieutenant Colonel in Samuel Jarvis' regiment, and of John Jarvis, First Lieutenant in an independent company stationed between Currituck and Roanoke inlets for the safeguard of the coast section, are also familiar to students of the Revolutionary history of our State; while in recent times ex-Governor Thomas Jarvis, in his services to the South during the War between the States, his educational campaign while Governor of North Carolina, his distinguished career as Minister to Brazil and as one of the most prominent members of the State Bar, has added further distinction to the honored name he bears.

Throughout the Revolution, from the Battle of Great Bridge, where her men fought gallantly in repelling Lord Dunmore's invasion, through the siege of Charleston, in the long and dreary winter at Valley Forge, on the fatal field of Camden, and in many other important crises of the war, the soldiers of Currituck were found in the front ranks of the American army, lustily shouting the "battle-cry of freedom." And not until the last British trooper had left our shores did they lay down their arms and return to their long neglected and deserted fields and farms.

But though the county gave freely of her sons to the American ranks, there were some within her borders who deserted the cause, and either openly or secretly sympathized with the enemy. The most noted of these Tories was Thomas McKnight, who showed his colors early in the struggle. McKnight was a prominent citizen of Indian Town. This colonial settlement was built on land reserved by the Lords Proprietors in 1704 to Yeopim Indians, whose chief town was called by them "Culong." In 1774 these Indians, with permission of the General Assembly, sold their lands, and with their king, John Durant, left the State. The lands were bought by Thomas McKnight, Gideon Lamb, Peter Daugé, Major Taylor Jones, John Humphries, William Ferebee, and Thomas Pool Williams, all Revolutionary soldiers or members of the legislative bodies before or after the war.

A white settlement grew up on the site of ancient "Culong," and the name of the red man's village was changed to Indian Town, in memory of its former inhabitants.

McKnight represented Currituck at the New Bern Convention of 1775, and there refusing to sign the document approving the Continental Congress at Philadelphia, and withdrawing from the Convention, he was accused of being a Tory by the House and denounced as a traitor to his country.

Though in an open letter to Joseph Jones, of Pasquotank, McKnight indignantly denied the charges against his loyalty to America, the Halifax Convention of 1770 ordered his estate to be confiscated and rented out for benefit of the State, by Isaac Gregory,

William Ferebee, and Abram Harrison. An amusing story is told of how McKnight acquired one of his plantations in Currituck. John Durant, the Chief of the Yeopims, had very astutely made it known to his own braves, as well as to his white neighbors, that the visions that visited him in his somnolent hours must somehow, somewhere, if within the range of possibility, materialize into visible, tangible realities, and that those who could, and did not help in their materialization, would incur the anger of the great chief. Now it was the habit of the wily red man, whenever he greatly desired to acquire a new possession, to dream that the owner of the coveted article had presented it to him. Having dwelt near the paleface for a number of years, the old chief adopted the white man's mode of dress to a certain extent. Needing, or coveting, a new coat, he very conveniently dreamed that McKnight, who had kept a trading store on Indian Ridge, gave him a bolt of bright cloth which appealed strongly to his innate love of bright colors. Presenting himself at the trader's store, he related his dream to the owner of the cloth; and McKnight not daring to incur the enmity of the Indian by refusing to let him have the coveted article, presented it to him forthwith; but McKnight, equally as shrewd as the chief, soon did some dreaming on his own account, and in his vision he saw himself the owner of some four hundred acres of land in Indian Ridge, the property of John Durant. So with due ceremony he approached the chief and solemnly related his dream; and the old Indian, realizing that in the Anglo-Saxon he had met his match—nay, his superior in cunning—made over to McKnight the land.

This plantation was afterwards bought by Doctor Marchant, a prominent citizen of Currituck, the friend and patron of Colonel Henry Shaw, whose gallant, though unsuccessful defense of Roanoke Island during the War between the States, brought honor and distinction to his native county.

Currituck in the past has played well her part in making the history of the Old North State, and that a bright and prosperous future awaits her may easily be seen by all who can read the signs of the times. Though nature on the one hand has placed many obstacles in the way of her progress by barring her coast to incoming vessels, and by surrounding her with barren shores and impenetrable marshes, on the other hand she has been abundantly generous to the ancient district. Where her marshes are drained, as in the region around Moyock, the richest corn land in the world is found. Her vast forests supply the great lumber mills of the Albemarle region; her sound and reedy shores provide her children with an abundance of fish and game, and with the completion of the Inland Waterway, which in Carolina follows the course of the old Albemarle and Chesapeake Canal, Currituck will be placed in closer touch with the great world from which she has so long been in a measure isolated. Material prosperity, far in excess of the homely comforts which her people have always enjoyed, will inevitably be the heritage of her children.

CHAPTER XV

EDENTON IN THE REVOLUTION

From the day when the war cloud of the Revolution first began to gather upon the American horizon, until the storm was spent and peace descended upon the land, the little coast town of Edenton played a conspicuous and heroic part in the struggle which for seven weary years wrought ruin and desolation throughout the thirteen Colonies.

As early as 1765, when the oppressive rule of England reached its culmination in the iniquitous Stamp Act, Edenton joined with the other Carolina towns in adopting resolutions expressing the strong indignation of her citizens at this act of tyranny on the part of George III and his Parliament. In 1773 three of her prominent citizens, Joseph Hewes, Samuel Johnston and Edward Vail, were appointed on the Carolina Committee of Correspondence which wrote to the other colonies that North Carolina was ready to join them against the King and Parliament. When England put into operation the famous Boston Port Bill and that sturdy little New England City was on the verge of starvation, Joseph Hewes, a merchant of Edenton, who was later to play a prominent part in Revolutionary events in North Carolina, joined with John Harvey, of Perquimans, in collecting supplies and provisions from the patriotic people of Albemarle, which they sent in the sloop Penelope to their distressed compatriots in far away Boston. Gratefully was the donation received by the inhabitants of that city, and a letter of thanks from the Boston committee amply repaid the donors for their generosity.

One of the earliest, and certainly one of the most interesting events in the Revolutionary annals of Edenton, was the far-famed Edenton Tea Party, held at the home of Mrs. Elizabeth King, on October 25, 1774. This famous gathering of the Edenton women was convened for the purpose of protesting against the tax on tea, which England had lately begun to extort from the colonies, and also for heartily endorsing the work of the first people's Convention, which, at the call of John Harvey, had met at New Bern in August, 1774.

Before the meeting adjourned these brave and patriotic women had drawn up resolutions firmly declaring their intention to drink no more of the taxed tea, and to uphold and encourage in every possible way the men of the colony in their struggle to gain all the rights due them as British subjects.

THE CUPOLA HOUSE, EDENTON, NORTH CAROLINA

The news of this bold stand of the Edenton women spread far and wide, and was commented upon by the newspapers of the day, both in America and England. Arthur Iredell, of London, brother of James Iredell, of Edenton, who married the sister of Samuel Johnston, on hearing of the event which seemed to have caused considerable stir in London, as well as throughout the thirteen Colonies, wrote to his brother from his home in London the following letter anent the affair:

"I see by the papers the Edenton ladies have signalized themselves by their protest against tea-drinking. The name of Johnston I see among them. Are any of my sister's relatives patriotic? I hope not, for we English are afraid of the male Congress; but if the ladies should attack us, the most fatal consequences are to be dreaded. So dextrous in the handling of a dart, each wound they give is mortal,

116

while we, so unhappily formed by nature, the more we strive to conquer them, the more we are conquered.

"The Edenton ladies, conscious of this superiority on their side by former experiences, are willing to crush us into atoms by their omnipotency. The only security on our side, to prevent impending ruin is the probability that there are few places in America which possess so much female artillery as Edenton. Pray let me know all the particulars when you favor us with a letter."

The old house under whose roof this historic Tea Party was held has only of recent years been destroyed. Age and decay undermined its walls, and it was found necessary to tear it down, but a handsome bronze tea-pot on an iron pedestal now marks the site of the ancient building; and within the halls of the State Capitol the Daughters of the Revolution have placed a bronze tablet in commemoration of this spirited act of the women of Edenton.

When John Harvey, of Perquimans, "The Father of the Revolution" in North Carolina died, his mantle fell upon Samuel Johnston, of Edenton, whose residence at "Hayes" now became the headquarters of the Whig party in North Carolina, and his office the rendezvous of the leaders of the patriots in the State, among whom Hewes, Iredell and Johnston, all of Edenton, stood foremost. So active were these three men in arousing and spreading the spirit of patriotism among their fellow-countrymen that McCree, in his "Iredell Letters," declares that "Much of the triumph at Moore's Creek must be ascribed to those three men, who at one time held frequent consultations in Johnston's office."

By the close of 1774, and the beginning of 1775, the flames of the Revolution, which had been slowly kindling, now burst into open conflagration, and Edenton began to experience something of the consequences of war.

Her militia had for some time been drilling, in preparation for the inevitable struggle; and Mrs. Iredell, in a letter to her husband, written in the spring of 1775, thus expresses the general anxiety and the apprehensive state of mind of the Edenton people: "The drum which is now beating while our soldiers exercise, drives every cheerful thought from my mind, and leaves it oppressed with melancholy reflections on the horrors of war."

In November of that year emissaries sent by Lord Dunmore, the Governor of Virginia, were discovered near the town, endeavoring to incite the slaves of that section to rise against their masters, murder them, and join the Tory army. But General Robert Howe, at the head of a detachment from his regiment, quickly drove these agents away, and thwarted the dastardly attempt; then marching on with six hundred North Carolina militia, into Virginia, the gallant General reached Norfolk two days after the victory of the patriots at Great Bridge, helped to expel Dunmore from Norfolk, and to take possession of the city for the Americans.

In April, 1776, the Halifax Convention authorized the delegates from North Carolina to the Continental Congress of that year, "to concur with the delegates of the other Colonies in declaring independence," and upon Joseph Hewes, of Edenton, fell the honor of presenting the Halifax Resolution of 1776 to the Congress at Philadelphia. To the instructions of the State he represented, Hewes added his own urgent plea for immediate action, and cast his State's vote squarely against postponing the declaration of independence. When the Continental Congress finally agreed to secede from the English Government, Hewes, with John Penn and William Hooper, of North Carolina, affixed his name to that famous document in which the thirteen Colonies foreswore their allegiance to King George.

Some two months after the Halifax Convention, and two weeks before the Continental Congress had formally declared independence, the vestry of Old St. Paul's Church in Edenton met in solemn conclave, and impelled by the wave of intense patriotism now sweeping over the land, drew up the so-called "Declaration of Independence of St. Paul's Parish," the context of which is as follows:

"We, the Subscribers, professing our Allegiance to the King, and acknowledging the Constitutional executive power of Government, do solemnly profess, testify and declare, that we do absolutely believe that neither the Parliament of Great Britain nor any member nor any Constituent Branch thereof, have a right to impose taxes upon these Colonies or to regulate the internal policy thereof; and that all attempts by fraud or force to establish and exercise such claims and powers are violation of the peace and security of the people, and ought to be resisted to the utmost, and the people of this Province singly and collectively are bound by the acts and resolutions of the Continental and Provincial Congresses, because in both they are freely represented by persons chosen by themselves, and we do solemnly and sincerely promise and engage under the sanction of virtue, honor, and the Sacred love of liberty and our country to maintain and support all and every acts, resolutions and regulations of the said Continental and Provincial Congresses to the utmost of our power and ability. In testimony whereof we have set our hands this 19th day of June, 1776."

During the winter of 1777 and 1778 nine battalions of soldiers from North Carolina were sharing with their comrades from the other colonies the hardships of those terrible months at Valley Forge. Half naked and starving, the soldiers would doubtless have given up the struggle to live through the awful winter, had not Governor Caswell, of North Carolina, energetically set about securing the needed supplies for the army. Joseph Hewes, responding generously to the call for help, sent his own ships to the West Indies to obtain necessaries for the army, had them brought to Edenton, and from there sent by wagon to Valley Forge.

After the American victory at Saratoga, France, who had been until then hesitating as to what course she should pursue in regard to helping the Americans against the ancient foe of the French, now yielded at last to Franklin's persuasions, and promised to send a large fleet and four thousand troops to aid the Colonies.

A party of French gentlemen, sympathizing with the Americans, and anxious to aid in the cause, came over to the States in advance of the army sent by the government, and landing in Edenton, were so agreeably impressed with the social life of the hospitable town, that they spent several weeks in the little metropolis. Three of these foreigners, Messieurs Pinchieu, Noirmont de la Neuville, and La Tours, seem to have made many friends in the town, and to have been the recipients of much hospitality on the part of the gentlefolk of Edenton.

Judge Iredell, who spoke French fluently, made a strong impression upon the strangers; and M. Pinchieu became one of his warm friends. The visit of the French officers to Edenton was made the

occasion of many social functions, and before the foreigners departed from the town, they gave a grand ball to the Edenton ladies, who
had made their stay so pleasant. The modest colonial maidens of
old Edenton, though dazzled and charmed by the airs and graces of
the gay and debonair strangers, at times found the manners of their
foreign guests a little too free for their comfort. Miss Nellie Blair, in
a letter to her uncle, Judge Iredell, declares most emphatically her
displeasure at the decidedly French behavior of one of her too atten-
tive foreign admirers.

On leaving Edenton, the Frenchmen proceeded to New Bern,
where they tendered their swords to the General Assembly, and
offered their services in the American cause; but for reasons not
stated their offer was declined.

The many acts of open rebellion on the part of prominent citizens
of Edenton had by this time made the town a marked spot in the
eyes of the enemy; and the fact that she was the most important port
in the Albemarle region, and that her destruction would be a heavy
blow to the entire State, also singled her out as an important point
of attack.

So in 1779, when Sir George Collier entered Hampton Roads, gut-
ted Norfolk, took possession of Portsmouth, and burned Suffolk, the
citizens of Edenton were thoroughly alarmed. The Dismal Swamp
was on fire, and the crackling of the burning reed resembling the
reports of musket shot, caused many to think that a battle was going
on near the town. Many of the inhabitants began to pack up their
household goods, ready to leave when the British should enter the
town.

But for some unknown reason the enemy, though so near, failed
to descend upon the town; and as days and weeks passed by, the
cloud of apprehension began to disperse, and life in the village to
resume its normal course.

Events, however, were to prove that the danger of invasion was
averted for a time only. In the fall of 1780, just after the disastrous
defeat of the Americans at Camden, and prior to Cornwallis' march
into North Carolina, General Leslie, of the British army, was sent
from New York to Virginia to keep the Americans in southeastern

Virginia and Albemarle from joining Greene's army in the effort to repel the invasion of Cornwallis.

Edenton was again in danger. The enemy, two thousand strong, were camped at Portsmouth, and one thousand were reported to have set out from Virginia on their way to attack the town. To add to the terror of the inhabitants, two British galleys, with sixty men each, had slipped through Roanoke Inlet, and were making for the little port. A letter from Mrs. Blair to James Iredell, written during those anxious days, gives a graphic description of conditions in Edenton at this juncture. "Vessels cannot get in," she writes; "two row galleys are between us and the bar, and are daily expected in Edenton. If they come, I do not know what we shall do. We are unable to run away, and I have hardly a negro well enough to dress us a little of anything to eat. We hear that there is an English fleet in Virginia, landing men at Kempe's."

Governor Nash, realizing that the town was in imminent danger, now ordered General Benbury, of Edenton, to join General Isaac Gregory at Great Swamp, near the Virginia border, and aid him in preventing General Leslie from entering Albemarle. At this post a battle was fought between Leslie's men and the militia under Benbury and Gregory, in which the latter were victorious. A little later Gregory wrote Governor Nash that Leslie's army had withdrawn from Virginia, but that he had not been able to ascertain the destination of the enemy. However, it soon became known that Leslie was hurrying to Camden, South Carolina, to join Cornwallis in his attempt to sweep through North Carolina and conquer that State, as he had conquered her sister State on the south.

With Leslie's army removed from the vicinity, Edenton remained for a few months free from the fear of invasion; but not for long did her citizens enjoy a respite from anxiety, for in January, 1781, the traitor, Benedict Arnold, was sent by the British to occupy the posts in Virginia lately deserted by Leslie. From Portsmouth Arnold wrote to General Sir Henry Clinton, K.C.B., that he was planning to send boats carrying five hundred men through Currituck Inlet, sweep the sound as high as Edenton, destroy that town and its shipping, and then proceed to New Bern, which he hoped to serve in like manner. Then he expected to post armed vessels outside

Currituck Inlet, distress the people of the coast country, and thus keep the people of eastern Carolina so busy defending their own homes that they would not be able to send men to interfere with the plans of Cornwallis.

Arnold asked Clinton for 100 ship carpenters to build the vessels necessary for the execution of his plans, but the traitor was not able to carry out his designs against the eastern towns, for on arriving in Virginia he found himself so hated and shunned by the British officers over whom he was placed that he soon resigned his command of the Virginia posts to General Phillips, of the British army, and instead of proceeding against Edenton, he undertook another expedition up the James River.

General Phillips, who now assumed command of the British in southeastern Virginia, immediately began to plan to join Cornwallis, who in the meantime had won the doubtful victory of Guilford Courthouse and had retreated to Wilmington.

The situation in Edenton was now alarming in the extreme. Leslie had 3,500 men in Virginia, 2,500 of whom, General Gregory wrote Iredell, had embarked at Kempe's Landing, supposedly for Edenton. Rumor had it that there were seven British boats at North Landing, and some at Knott's Island. Cornwallis' Army was marching northward from Wilmington, and reports from nearby counties that lay in his path, told of the atrocious crimes committed by his men against women and children, of devastated fields and homes burned and ruined. Hundreds of negroes were foraging for the British army, and the Tories everywhere were wreaking vengeance upon their Whig neighbors.

The long dreaded day at last arrived. Edenton was raided, and the vessels in her harbor burned and carried off. Eden House, some ten miles from the town, the home of Robert Smith, a prominent merchant of Edenton, was plundered, and valuable papers destroyed. Many of the beautiful homes of the planters in the neighborhood were destroyed, and a schooner belonging to Robert Smith, and one, the property of a Mr. Littlejohn, were captured by the enemy and carried off down the sound.

The danger was so real that many families fled from the town and sought refuge in Windsor, and the homes of that hospitable little village were crowded with women and children. But in spite of the discomfort that host and guest alike must have suffered from the overflow of visitors, the letters of the refugees to their husbands and fathers in Edenton speak in warm praise of the cheerfulness and good humor that prevailed in the little town during those trying and anxious days, and of the merry social gatherings held in honor of the guests.

Though panic-stricken at first when confronted by the long apprehended danger, the citizens soon rallied and bravely resisted the foe. Charles Johnson, writing to James Iredell, says: "The inhabitants in general and the sailors, have and do turn out unanimously. I never saw nor could I hope to see so much public spirit, personal courage and intrepid resolution." Robert Smith's schooner was retaken from the enemy, and later the Row Galley that had invaded Edenton and captured the schooners was taken, and her commander, Captain Quinn, lodged in Edenton jail.

In the meantime the refugees at Windsor were beginning to doubt their wisdom in leaving their homes for the Bertie town. Many of them were afraid that they had only jumped from the frying-pan into the fire. Cornwallis was only thirty miles away, in Halifax, and the Windsor people were in daily terror that foraging parties from his army would descend upon their homes. To add to the danger of their situation, the hated and dreaded Arnold, whose expedition up the James had been attended by the perpetration of many dastardly cruelties, was marching south to join Cornwallis in Carolina. Six hundred negroes, sent by Cornwallis, were near Edenton, and other bands of foragers, two thousand in all, were pillaging and plundering in the wake of the British army.

Fortunately for Edenton and the adjacent towns, Anthony Wayne was stationed at Roanoke with his troops. Hearing of the ravages committed by Cornwallis' men, he marched in pursuit of the enemy, who now left North Carolina, entered Virginia, burned South Quays, and then proceeded on their way to Yorktown.

In June, 1781, Samuel Johnston, of Edenton, was elected delegate to the Continental Congress, the first that had assembled since the adoption of the Articles of Confederation. His high ability and acknowledged statesmanship won for him in that body the distinguished honor of being elected to the office of President of Congress. But the critical situation in Edenton, and his anxiety concerning his family, decided him to decline the office and return home to share the fortunes of his townsmen and to render what aid he could to his own people.

In August, 1781, Charles Johnson wrote Governor Burke that a French fleet had appeared off the Virginia Capes, and had driven back General Leslie; and General Gregory, who had been stationed at Edmund's Hill in Nansemond County, Virginia, to hold Leslie in check, reported at the same time that the enemy had evacuated Portsmouth, and that it was useless to keep his soldiers there any longer.

The British army had by this time reached Yorktown, where, on the 19th of October the famous surrender took place, and the long, weary struggle for independence was over; but it was nearly a month later before the joyful news of Washington's victory over Cornwallis reached Carolina. On November 18th the British troops in the State embarked from Wilmington, and North Carolina was troubled by the red-coats no more.

But though the surrender at Yorktown had convinced the British that she had lost her hold upon the American Colonies, it was not until September, 1782, that the King acknowledged the independence of his former American subjects; and still another year passed before the Treaty of Paris was signed, formally acknowledging the United States a separate and independent power.

During these two years North Carolina was torn and harrassed by bands of Tories; and in South Carolina the armies of Greene and Leslie were still engaged in fierce skirmishes. Leslie was at last hemmed in at Charleston by Greene's troops, and both his men and Greene's soldiers were in great distress for want of food and clothing.

In the summer of 1782 Greene warned the people of North Carolina that the British in Charleston were preparing to send four vessels to raid Edenton, New Bern and Wilmington; and once more the inhabitants of these towns were plunged into a state of alarm.

Governor Burke immediately ordered General Gregory to have 500 men ready to march at a moment's notice to Edenton to repel the expected invasion, and also ordered him to ask the merchants of Edenton how many vessels they thought necessary to protect the town. The Governor furthermore gave Gregory instructions to purchase cannon and to draft men to man the boats, guaranteeing, himself, full pay for men and supplies.

But the fleet of which Greene had written did not arrive, though during the summer of 1782, Tory galleys appeared in the bay and kept the town in constant terror of another raid. The fall passed without bringing the expected invasion, and finally the joyful news came that on December 14th the British had evacuated Charleston, and that their fleet had sailed for the North.

With the departure of the British fleet and army from the South, all fear of further invasion was over, and the little town of Edenton settled down to long years of peace and happiness.

FINIS